Swimming for Our Lives

Swimming for Our Lives

A Naval Academy Graduate's Stories of an Adventurous Life

James D Paulk Jr.

BOOKLOGIX

Alpharetta, GA

ISBN: 978-1-6653-0416-0 - Paperback
ISBN: 978-1-6653-0415-3 - Hardcover
eISBN: 978-1-6653-0585-3 - ePub

Library of Congress Control Number: 2022920078

Printed in the United States of America   1 1 2 2 2 2

⊗This paper meets the requirements of ANSI/NISO Z39.48-1992 (Permanence of Paper)

PAT

My partner, best friend, and the love of my life.

Contents

Foreword

T HE LOVE AND ADMIRATION between a father and daughter are often uniquely special and hard to put into words. As the first-born child, when I was old enough, I was often the one to wake up before the sunrise to head out on a fishing adventure with my dad. My younger siblings, Tom and Linda, were also born into a lifetime of endless fishing, boating, and adventures that we shared as a family, along with numerous family friends. These memories have provided not only our father but us as well, with countless stories to pass down to future generations.

As most adventure seekers know, great fishing and travel excursions can turn from fun and exciting, to ominous, and a need to find a quick solution. Readers will find in this book the several scary and thrilling experiences dad faced with his friends— whether it was during his years serving in the Navy, fishing, or other adventures, things quickly evolved and turned into a matter of *Swimming for Our Lives*.

What I have admired most about my father is his lifetime of passion to serve his country, the communities that he lived in, and the churches that he worshiped in. No matter what he participated in, dad was frequently asked to take on a leadership role within several organizations, because he had the exceptional talent of leadership, motivating others, and providing hands-on direction.

You will see a trend throughout this book, that my father's unique style of leadership is by building a successful team. Whether it be related to organizing a simple fishing charter, a fishing conservation initiative, or a fund-raising effort, he always gives credit to the team involved. Or as he likes to refer to it "a WE effort!"

Dad's integrity and loyalty to those he loves, and passion for living life to the fullest have made an indelible impression on my life. I am eternally grateful for the example of his love of God, his family, and his country.

—Pam Paulk Minor

Introduction

Y OU MIGHT ASK, "Why this book?" and so, I'll tell you. My life has been full of fun and adventure. While I was employed by a large corporation for most of my life, there was always time for vacations, activities, and adventures! Recently I have been reflecting on those activities and adventures. Some were significant events etched into my memory. Some adventures were brief, others were not, but all became a part of the fabric of my life.

The title of the book, *Swimming for Our Lives*, came naturally because several stories directly relate to this experience. So, there it is! I want to share my memories of those and other adventures with my friends, family, and descendants. Yes, I have related many of these tales to my family while waiting for dessert after holiday dinners—but there are folks yet to come who might like to know more about Ole Jim and who he was and what he did! So, I have written them down and assembled this book for those who have not (and for those who have) been present for my various tellings.

The stories here are not in chronological or any specific order. Many are about fishing, or somewhat related to fishing, because fishing was a passion in my life, always present and always a plan. When I was a lad, seven to eight years old, I tied some thread to a bamboo pole and bent a straight pin into a hook. This rig, with some bread rolled into a ball and put on my make-shift hook, helped me catch three-inch bullhead minnows! That thrill as a youngster hooked me for life.

This book documents a few things about me, my family, and my friends so readers of current or future generations can smile, shed a tear, or, at worst, shake their heads at us. At the very least they will know more than just the dates of when we were born and when we died. We really existed! We worked on many things and even accomplished some of them. Hopefully, our contributions to our society were useful and, maybe, even significant. We'd like to think that we made the world a better place because we were here, and the biggest hope of all is that we inspire future generations to do the same.

SWIMMING FOR OUR LIVES

———

S OMETIMES THINGS DON'T TURN OUT the way you thought they would. Sometimes they turn out to be downright scary.

It started out to be a very simple, short trip—no fishing, just a couple of hours at low tide to get a bucket or two of oysters to go with the fish that evening for a fish fry at a hunting camp. Creating any excuse for a big, more complete, eating event is something that we are good at in the south, but I'm getting ahead of myself.

It was December—an important fact for you to remember. My wife and I had arrived only a few hours earlier in coastal Georgia following a cross-country flight from California for a visit with my brother, Bobby, and other kinfolks. Shortly after dinner, Bobby's adult son, Skipper, and his best friend, Terry, walked in the front door in their heavy-duty camos (it had been cold in the woods).

"Where have you guys been," Bobby asked. "Are you hungry?"

"Yes sir." What did you expect? Boys are always hungry!

"Did you have any luck?"

"Yes, sir, that's why we are so late. It took us over two hours to find the deer."

"How big was it?"

"Six points." Well, you get the idea. Bobby's wife, Vila, warmed up the leftovers for the starving hunters who proceeded to shovel it down—it had been a long day.

Then, the talk turned to the next day and the potential Friday night fish fry. Bobby said, "It sure would be nice if we had some oysters to go along with the fried fish, hush puppies, slaw, and other good fixings, wouldn't it?"

Skipper spoke up first and noted that it was low tide at eight in the morning, but he couldn't go because of an appointment. "I can go, but I have to be back by 10," Terry said.

Bobby said, "Okay, let's meet at the St. Marys' launching ramp at seven." We were ready for a quick excursion to get some raw oysters to shuck and enjoy, mm, mm, good. No big deal, right?

At seven the next morning, we arrived at the St. Mary's downtown launching ramp where we saw no other parked boat rigs.

Bobby got into Terry's truck and backed the trailer into the water as Terry was already there, ready to put the boat in the water.

Since there was no other boat activity at the ramp, Terry ran the bow of the boat up on the ramp instead of taking the boat to the floating dock. He then pulled the bow farther up using the anchor rope—a key point in this story.

With Terry at the stern seat to run the motor, I got into the middle seat, and Bobby pushed us off and jumped into the front seat.

In the downtown area with a nearby marina, other docks, and moorings, boats were required to maintain a slow speed in a "no-wake zone." So, we started down the St. Mary's River very slowly, as required. Loaded with a rake, a couple of five-gallon buckets, and a cooler, we had all we needed for raking up the oysters and getting back by ten.

When we cleared the "no-wake zone," Terry accelerated to get us to the creek quickly where we could find some safe, edible oysters exposed at the low tide. There were other creeks we had to avoid where chemicals had been discharged from manufacturing sites, contaminating the oysters there.

However, another key point is that St. Mary's is a wide river that is the dividing line between Georgia and Florida. On this trip, we were in a flat bottom, shallow draft boat capable of allowing us to get far enough up the creek to find the safe oysters so important to us.

With the boat running wide open to get us to our destination, we were in good spirits, joking around as always, holding onto our hats. Now, I may have mentioned that this was in December, and so, we had on winter jackets and a couple of shirts to keep ourselves warm with either boots or tennis shoes on.

Suddenly, I felt like I was falling overboard. My mind was very fuzzy, like in a dream, but no way could this be happening. I was firmly seated in the middle of the boat, yet, I was really in the water. *This was stupid. How could I be in the water? They'll be turning the boat around to pick me up and laughing like crazy.*

However, when I got my wits together, I turned my head around to look for the boat, and there it was, twenty to thirty yards away going around in a circle with my brother holding on to a rope for dear life near the bow. Looking in another direction, there was Terry, he was in the water too. No one was in the boat! This was impossible.

Now, I had to decide, swim to the boat or swim to the marsh? I knew that whatever I chose, I had to start quickly. We were right in the middle of a very wide river, with no other boats in sight. The cooler, life jackets, and other items were floating swiftly out to sea in the fast, outgoing current. Since the distance to the boat appeared to be closer than the marsh, I set out swimming the best that I could with a winter coat and tennis shoes on. I was struggling to make headway. Bobby looked like a circus performer as he went around and around, holding onto that rope to keep from being run over by the boat propeller.

Before I could get to the boat, fortunately, Terry got into it and shut down the motor. Bobby and I were extremely lucky that a young man was with us who could swim to the boat with boots on and get into the boat neither of us could. After Terry bailed out the boat, that had a considerable amount of water in it with a five-gallon bucket that somehow did not go over the side, he ran the boat into the marsh with Bobby and me hanging on opposite sides so we could stand up enough to pull ourselves into the boat. Terry saved our lives, no doubt about it, for without his help, Bobby and I would never have survived.

Now what? With our tails tucked appropriately between our legs, we quickly decided that the oyster hunt was over. We headed back to the launching ramp, soaking wet, a little cold, but alive. We never saw another boat on the water that morning. Bobby and I decided that it was a good thing that our father wasn't with us, he couldn't swim and would have drowned for sure. It was all that we could do to save ourselves, much less save him too.

Now, how could this have happened? We didn't hit anything floating in the water or run over a mud bank. It took us a while to figure it out, but seeing the rope in the water, was a big clue.

Here is what we decided happened: When the boat speed increased, a small bit of rope remained in the water when we left the boat ramp which, unseen by us, was completely pulled out of the boat. Since it was tied to the bow at one end and to the anchor in the boat at the other end, a large loop formed in the water. This loop acted like a brake on the boat's port (left) side and flipped it—and us—over into the water. Fortunately, the boat righted itself, but with a lot of water in it.

When we got back with this story, we couldn't lie as wet as we were, and we quickly became the butt of many jokes, although our group was happy that we survived. When my brother went back to work, there was a big ceremony at which he was presented with a life jacket. Being alive was important, but we had to laugh at ourselves too. It was another crazy incident in our lives that became etched in our minds. We cheated death that day for sure.

AN ADVENTURE OF OUR YOUTH

———

W HEN WE MENTION that we have a Baja California story, those from southern California start to smile because, although some are tragic, most are very funny. Folks from other areas say "huh?" and have no idea what the story will entail. This is a "Baja" story which—by definition—is an adventure to be told over and over. Anyone who has traveled to Baja probably has at least one similar story to tell, and I hope that you get as much of a kick out of reading this as I do remembering the fun that we had.

This trip was in January 1970, just a few months after our family moved to California. The leader of our expedition was Ron Fipps, a mechanical manager at Procter and Gamble in Long Beach where all four of us worked. Travis Rushing and Pat Connelly were two young engineers who had recently graduated from the University of Arizona, and I was Soap Operations Manager at the time.

We planned to drive down to Gonzaga Bay, about 120 miles south of San Felipe on the Baja California peninsula, where the paved road ended. Gonzaga was on the Sea of Cortez which separates the Baja peninsula from mainland Mexico. We planned to camp and fish for white seabass which can grow to thirty to fifty pounds. The totoaba (the largest member of the croaker family also) was pretty much gone by then, but there was always a chance that we could catch one of these larger croakers weighing over a hundred pounds. That's the way fishermen think—and believe me, we had those kinds of dreams.

In preparation for the trip, Pat Connelly bought a ten-year-old, beat-up minivan that had a forty-hp motor. Can you see the beginning of our problems? It had two seats in the front and none in the back, so the seating for two of us was either on the floor or in a lawn chair, but we were young, so this didn't bother us at the time. Of course, we weren't as wise as we are now.

I volunteered to bring a set of tools, but Connelly said that he had his own great set and insisted upon bringing them (more on the tools later). He also wanted to bring his motorcycle, but with a small wooden boat tied down on top of the van, an outboard motor, extra fuel, extra water, a tent, fishing gear, sleeping bags, beer, wine, rum, supplies, etc., we finally convinced him we didn't have room for his bike. And as it turned out, this was one of our better decisions.

For some reason, I started a log on our trip. Maybe it was my Navy background, I had recently found my notes and thought, as I said before, others might get a chuckle from our memories about these misadventures in Baja.

We left Ron's house on a Friday afternoon in January 1970 at 1:50 p.m. and then we left *again* at 2:10. We had to go back to get the tent stakes. How's that for a start? As we left the house again, we hoped we hadn't forgotten anything else, but we were so excited about the prospects of all the big fish we were going to catch that almost nothing else was on our minds. At 4:00 p.m., we had to stop for gas, and as we neared El Centro, California, near the border, we were already having problems going up hills and fighting strong headwinds on the freeway. It was obvious that our overloaded and underpowered van was a problem—it was a good thing that we were not in an airplane, or we'd have been history! *Crash, bang,* DOA!

We stopped in El Centro for our last meal before entering Mexico, and that's when we discovered the "wine disaster." A half-a-gallon bottle of red wine had broken in the back of the van, and we had a good laugh as we cleaned up the mess. Lost was a lot of good liquid that we had planned for the nine-day trip. Ugh!

After crossing the border, we went through Mexicali, which sits on the Mexico side of the border, at about 9:30 p.m., and traveled down the paved road to San Felipe, arriving there at 12:30 a.m., not a bad transit time for us. The next sixty-mile trip on an unpaved and non-maintained road to Puertecitos was another story. In the dark, we were stopped on this dirt road in the middle of nowhere by Federales to check us for guns. Being flagged down by these bandito-looking guys with lanterns and semiautomatic rifles was as scary as it gets. Think about it!

They surrounded us, and we listened while Ron convinced them to let us go after a cursory inspection. The road was so bad, it was dangerous to go too fast. By the time we reached Puertecitos— five hours later—we were so exhausted that we pulled the van off the road, pulled out our sleeping bags, and slept for a couple of hours on the ground. After refueling at our last possible place with an ancient, hand-cranked gas pump on top of a fifty-five-gallon drum in Puertecitos, we continued our trip south.

The road was awful, with lots of potholes, ruts, and deep, desert sand on either side of the road. Ron told Connelly, who did most of the driving, that if we hit a pothole, he shouldn't let go of the steering wheel. Five minutes later, we hit a big pothole and— you guessed it—Connelly let go of the steering wheel! Something didn't feel right. After getting out to check, our right front tire was turned sideways while the tire on the other side was going straight. Wow! We had bent a tie rod!

Ron said, "Connelly, now is the time to break out that great set of tools that you brought." Well, it turned out he had a ball-peen hammer, a pair of pliers, and a big screwdriver with a broken wooden handle. After a half-hour, Ron magically had the tie rod out, and we pounded it with a rock and hammer. FUN, FUN, FUN!

With another admonition to hold onto the wheel, we were underway again after losing only thirty-five minutes. Less than an hour later, we came to a small, beautiful, isolated beach, and decided to put up the tent, make camp, and prepare our first meal. We fished until dark and caught about fifteen to twenty fish, the largest being a three-pound perch. What a great relief to be fishing at last, even if there was nothing remarkable about our catch. After a great steak dinner, we slept for ten hours—it had been a long, exhausting trip to this point.

Sunday morning, after a breakfast of pancakes and sausage, our rested group of guys broke camp and headed south again. We anticipated an early afternoon arrival in Gonzaga—a trip of only about fifty miles. Little did we know the problems ahead. Our van stalled on the first significant mountain road that had a notoriously dangerous and narrow, curving, steep slope with a cliff to the right and mountainside to the left of us. So, we removed as much of our load as we could and three of us pushed until the van stalled again. We hastily put a rock under a rear tire to keep it from rolling down the mountain and got the engine going again. We pushed until it stalled again.

Then, disaster. Before we could get a rock under the wheel, the van went flying by us, heading down the curving mountain slope backward. As he went by, Connelly was yelling, "I lost the brakes!" We chased the minivan down the mountain, hoping it wouldn't go over the cliff. (There was a pile of cars at the bottom of the cliff, so, it was obvious that this had happened before.) But, before the van could go over, it hit a large rock and almost turned over. Fortunately, we had loaded most of our things on the left side of the van, and this extra weight kept it from turning over.

It scared the Hell out of us as we raced down the hill after it. When the van finally came to rest, we got to Connelly. He was okay, but we had to pry his fingers off the steering wheel, and he was white as a sheet! This had been a very scary situation, and we didn't know what had happened, or what we were going to do. No one else was around. This was about as remote a location as you could find.

Our investigation turned up a broken brake cylinder line in the left front wheel. Apparently, when the brakes were replaced before we left on this trip, the mechanic had over-tightened the three-inch-long copper tubing elbow, twisting it in the path of the brake cylinder, which had finally cut through the copper tubing, causing a loss of the brake fluid. Now, what would we do? We decided our best option was to block off the brake on that wheel and have brakes on the other three, but after climbing down the hillside and checking all the wrecks down there, none of them had a metric bolt. Unfortunately, all were American cars. We started examining our van and found a metric bolt on the steering column that would fit. So, after putting it in place and replacing the lost brake fluid, we were on our way again.

Without Ron's talent, we might still be wandering around the desert in Baja! He had saved us again. After pushing the van back up to the top of the mountain, and hauling the gear up, we had a round of beers. After all, we were exhausted and covered in sweat! Then, when we went down the backside of the mountain, we had to do the drill all over again to go up the next one. We brought enough supplies to last us for the entire trip because where we were going, there was nothing. Imagine us hauling five-gallon containers of gas and water, an outboard motor, and heavy items to the tops of those two mountains.

At the top of the second mountain, there was a beautiful little shrine about three feet tall, with coins and other items for the Holy Mother. We couldn't help but notice that we had made sixteen miles in five hours—not what we expected when we left camp that morning. But, after our troubles and surviving them, like the Mexicans before us, we left a few coins at the shrine too. We were thankful to be alive.

We had one more mountain to surmount. We had to push the

van to the top and then, we had to go back down the mountain, get the gear and bring it back to the top. Finally, we arrived at Papa Fernandez's Fish Camp in Gonzaga at 4:45 p.m. What a way to spend a Sunday. It was a wonder that none of us had a heart attack or something, maybe the beer saved us! Papa had three or four plywood cabins and gave us the nicest one *en la playa* (on the beach) with a picnic table in front of it. It had a beautiful view, but with rather rugged accommodations. To us, it was a five-star hotel.

For dinner, we had tacos, beans, and beer. After no lunch and only beer during our seven-and-a-half-hour trip of fifty miles, Ron fixed us a super dinner. The best news of all was that we were going fishing in the morning, can you imagine how excited we were? About to jump clean out of our skin! No mountains tomorrow! Only the Sea of Cortez and white seabass to wrestle with.

We were up at 4:30 in the morning and underway by 6:00. Naturally, our guide, Francisco, had trouble getting the motor going. Always happens, right? As we neared our island destination though, we could smell the wildflowers. All our troubles were behind us . . . hopefully.

At 8:30, I caught my very first white seabass of the trip, a thirty-five pounder. Man, I was in heaven! We caught four WSB and some smaller fish. We were fishing with white candy-bar-shaped jigs on the bottom, jerking them to make them look like squid. The fishing day was cut short when the wind picked up around noon, and we couldn't risk any rough weather in the open panga boat, with no other boats in the vicinity to come to our rescue, no life jackets, and no radio either. Coast Guard wouldn't even be able to help us down here. So, by 11:30, fishing was over for the day and we were back in camp before 1:00 p.m.

Our guide, Francisco, joined us for dinner that evening. It consisted of rum drinks, white seabass, corn, and potatoes. It was excellent, and we joked it was probably the best meal Francisco had ever had—having lived in this remote location his whole life. We didn't know yet, but it was to be the best of our trip too.

Tuesday was just like Monday: underway early, and we caught a couple of fish. Then it started to rain and more motor trouble (the spark plug wire was broken). By the middle of the day, we had caught a couple more and headed back in with a stormy sea, rain, and a little wind chop on the water.

Papa Fernandez had told Ron that our palapa on the beach (*la playa*) would leak if it rained, and we would need to move to another one that had a better roof on it. Of course, it started to rain again just before dinner, but nothing was coming through the roof. We joked that maybe Papa was wrong about the roof.

Suddenly, the rain came pouring through, and within seconds, we had a half inch of water in there. We grabbed our sleeping bags and air mattresses and ran for another cabana, laughing all the way. It seemed Papa knew what he was talking about.

Papa and his family had been running the camp forever and was in his late seventies then and, believe it or not, he was still alive when I first wrote this story. As best as I can determine, he lived to be over a hundred years old. Rocks and debris had been cleared in his area so that small planes could land there to take him north for medical issues, and the pilots could fish there without venturing over the dangerous mountain roads. Quite a guy, we were impressed with the way he created a unique way of life.

We fixed burritos for dinner and started worrying about the condition of the road due to the rain. We could be stuck there for days and money, food, and our water supply were already getting low. We ran out of rum on Monday night and only had one bottle of wine left—you may remember, we lost a half-gallon of red wine in the van miscue. Papa had *cerveza* in the cantina, so all was not lost.

Sleeping on Tuesday night was a problem because the air was leaking out of three of the four air mattresses. The concrete floor of the cabana was hard, but we were young and handled it with more laughs. This was quite an adventure for us, to say the least.

We were up early again on Wednesday and moved our gear back over to the wet cabana, with only coffee for breakfast. It was a pretty sunrise after the rain, as only one in Baja can be. It was a little windy, but the seas were calm. We persuaded Ron to serenade us on the way out. He had a great baritone voice, and the boat motor wasn't running very well either—probably due to the rain. The mountains had turned green after the rain and were in stark contrast with the surrounding desert area. It was beautiful. We caught a few small fish on bait and lost two seabass, but by noon the water became choppy, and we headed in.

Thursday, we woke up late with no time to fix sandwiches, only leftover coffee for breakfast. The motor wouldn't run again, and we had nothing to do but paddle back in to get another motor. The shaft of the next motor was too short, but we finally got the original one going. Around noon, we started catching WSB after a rather poor start for the day, and we ended up with four WSB. On the way back, we stopped a passing shrimp boat to buy ice to preserve our fish during our trip home and to keep them on ice in Papa's little icehouse.

Papa previously had told us that the front end of a van like ours was buried on the beach, so we decided to look for it and—wonder of all wonders—after poking sticks in the sand, we found it! We dug it up, found a replacement copper tubing that was a perfect fit, and fixed our brakes. Now we had brakes on all four wheels. We also put in four new spark plugs, a new set of points, a condenser, etc., and made plans for leaving Friday morning. Somehow it seemed too soon to be heading home, though. Despite all our problems, we were having a ball.

Friday morning, we left Papa and Gonzaga Bay behind and made good time across the desert (the roads turned out to be fine) and started our "push the van up the mountain" routine when we got to the mountains. Our mouths got so dry, our tongues tended to stick to the roof of our mouths. If our beer had run out, we might have died. We made good time, though, and were at Puertecitos by noon and at San Felipe by 3:30 p.m.

We reached the border around dark, and when the customs officers saw us (we hadn't shaved or bathed in nine days and probably looked like bums), they asked us to get out of the van and unload it for inspection. We had the white seabass tightly wrapped inside the tent canvas with ice to get them home safely and dreaded unwrapping them. But, after talking with us for a few minutes, they started laughing and told us to pack up and get out of there. Sympathetic, I guess! We stopped in El Centro for dinner after only having a couple of beers since breakfast (twelve hours).

After filling up on gas, we headed for home and finally got to Ron's house at 2:30 a.m. Our trip home had been a lot smoother than our trip down, but all in all, we had created some memories that would last a lifetime. We caught some nice fish every day and, most importantly all things considered, we came back alive! Unfortunately, gillnets have ruined the fishing at Gonzaga Bay now, and WSB are mostly gone, but I did hear that someone caught a totoaba over a hundred pounds there a few years ago, but the days of great WSB fishing are over.

After this trip, Ron and I became close friends, our friendship lasted until his untimely death, and I never ceased to be amazed at his incredible talent. As for Papa, he's gone now too, but if you get in the neighborhood, stop by to see his camp and have a beer in his cantina. He was a special guy who created a special camp out of nothing, a great place to fish and visit.

At the time of this trip, I didn't know any of these guys very well, but after working, socializing, and vacationing together for many years, Ron and I became best of friends, almost like brothers. He's without a doubt the most talented person that I've ever known. He sang lead roles with the Long Beach Civic Light Opera, he was a great storyteller, a fabulous cook, a pilot, spoke excellent Spanish, was an incredible mechanic, and could fix anything. He was also an inventor; well, you get the idea. Unfortunately, Ron passed away years ago and many of the plans that we had made for our retirement years never came to fruition. He is dearly missed.

Four happy anglers
with white seabass.

Man in Boat – Our
guide, Francisco.

Minivan – On the way to Gonzaga Bay.

KONA BLUES

B LUES? AS IN BLUE MARLIN, anyway. Pat, neighbors Bud and Marcene Galli, and I left the Los Angeles airport on an afternoon in late March on a direct flight to Kona with a planeload of passengers that included many very excited students on their spring break. We knew that their goal was a lot different from ours, likely returning to school with a good tan was at the top of their list. It was a long flight, and since we were fishing the next morning, we couldn't help but think "by this time tomorrow, we could be hooked up to a big one." We were also excited, and even though we have both been fishing for well over fifty years, an adventure was anticipated. One never knows what experience will be added to a list of life-long tales to be told and retold.

Adding to the excitement of the trip was the addition of four special lures to test on the Kona fishing grounds. We had acquired two Seven Strand electronic, acoustical lures (EAL's) rigged with skirts suitable for Kona, and two lures that Ken Verkerk had selected for our trip from his Hi-5 booth at the Fred Hall Fishing Show. The Seven Strand EAL's came out in 2001, and though they haven't been widely distributed, those fishermen who have used them have given them credit for their success, especially during the southern California tournament season. Wherever they have been used, the feedback has been positive. The lures have a microchip that emits the sound of a wounded mackerel and is powered by a three-volt lithium battery that lasts for about a day of trolling. An expensive battery, but everything about offshore fishing is expensive, fuel especially. In an issue of *Fish Taco Chronicles*, we not only gave a detailed evolution of the acoustical lure but gave it kudos for the sailfish we caught in Zihuatanejo over a Thanksgiving holiday trip to Mexico.

Hi-5 Custom Lures were new to us. Ken Verkerk, the owner, said that Hi-5 is the culmination of his desire to create a lure that runs in a balanced fashion with the swimming action he was looking for. After less than five years in the business, he was shipping custom lures to anglers around the world.

Making travel arrangements today is an easier process than it used to be. For accommodations, a brief call to World Mark the Club, and we were all set for a week in a two-bedroom condo for midweek arrival and departure located on Alii Drive, a short distance from downtown Kailua-Kona. E-tickets bought on the internet let us avoid the long lines at LAX, and we printed our boarding passes—that's progress. For fishing charters, we emailed Capt. Jerry Allen, and after a couple of queries, we locked in two days on the *Sea Dancer*, a boat we had fished before.

As for things to do in Kona, when you aren't fishing every day, there is much to choose from. We have been visiting the Hawaiian Islands for over thirty years, and Kona is our favorite. A free booklet you can find everywhere, *101 Things to Do on the Big Island*, will provide you with lots of ideas. Over the years, we have gone snorkeling from the Fairwind at Capt. Cook's Inlet, took a helicopter flight over Kilauea's volcano erupting vent, attended a luau (tried poi, but didn't care for it), and toured most of the tourist sights on the island.

After arriving at the Kona airport and picking up a rental car, we stopped at the local Safeway on Henry Street to get sandwich makings for the next day. It was late, and we were worried the store and the World Mark office would be closed, but our fears turned out to be unwarranted. We made it, and with an early start in the morning, we couldn't miss a meal, could we? After throwing the sandwiches together, and unpacking, we hit the sack for a few hours of sleep prior to a day we knew was going to be a good one. We had come a long way, and we had four special lures that were going to work miracles for us.

We got to Honokaa Marina, the small boat harbor, before 7:00 a.m., an hour before most boats leave. Captain Jerry wanted to get a head start on the other boats, and the engines on the *Sea Dancer* were already running as we scrambled over the transom with our gear. John Akina, Jerry's mate for over ten years, gave us a helping hand and, after a brief greeting, the boat was out of the slip and gliding out of the harbor. In less than ten minutes, we were in deep, beautiful blue water, and we had our lures out. We were fishing. There was no wind, a little swell running, low clouds on the horizon, and a blue sky overhead. It looked like another beautiful day in paradise.

As we passed over the thousand-fathom drop-off, Jerry put the boat on autopilot, rigged our four lures, and got them in the water. Our lure evaluation was now in progress, and we noticed that, in the distance, other boats were starting to come out of the harbor. Hopefully, we were going to get the first shot at a fish.

After an hour and a half of trolling our special lures, we had settled down into a relaxed state of anticipation, and we couldn't help but notice there were fifteen to twenty other boats scattered around the area, most off on the horizon. Suddenly, Jerry shouted, "port rigger!" There was a big swirl but no hookup, not even a zip. We were now wide-awake. Jerry sped up and slowed down the boat to entice the big fish to try again, but no luck. So, he circled the boat back to the spot where the fish first came up, and then, all hell broke loose. The big marlin ate the Hi-5 "flying fish" lure on the center stinger behind a bird teaser. We were only five miles off the beach.

The blue marlin took off like she was in a race. The eighty-pound test line was screaming off the spool as if there was no drag, but the drag on the Penn International 80W was set at twenty-pounds. Then she came up, jumping at five hundred yards behind the boat. Jerry said, "It's a big one! Probably five to six hundred pounds." I had several thoughts going through my mind, all at the same time. Ten years previously, I fought a 317-pound blue for two hours on a fifty-pound line standing up, darned near killed me and now, this one looked bigger.

At least I was in the fighting chair with the reel strapped to a back harness, but I was still thinking, *Do I really want to do this?* I was also watching the line melt off the reel, all the monoline was in the water, and the Dacron backing line looked to me as though it had never been off the spool before. I thought there was a good chance we were going to get spooled (lose all line to the fish). Of course, the boat was on autopilot, and Captain Jerry, John, and Bud, our next-door neighbor in California who had joined us with his wife for this vacation, were getting the other rods safely stowed and, in my mind, were taking their time about it! So, I turned to Jerry and anxiously said, "We better get after this fish pretty quick, or I'm either going to get spooled or go into the water too."

Jerry calmly climbed back up to the flybridge and calmly started backing down—not too fast, just enough to help me get a few more wraps on the spool. John, in the meantime, took up a position behind the chair and kept it pointed in the direction of the fish, and gave me encouragement and instructions. In all my years of big game fishing, it had been done in a standing position. I was not used to the rhythm of leaning forward in the chair and using my back rather than my arms to lift the rod. John said, "If you only use your arms, she'll beat you in no time." He was right, and I started using my back and using short strokes, and the line slowly began to fill what had formerly looked like an empty spool.

Now as I started to think about all the line I would need to retrieve before we got the fish to the boat, Jerry looked down from the bridge and said, "Can you believe that people pay good money to work this hard?" He was smiling, and I smiled back and shook my head, but I was sweating pretty good, and my mouth was dry.

"Bud, will you please get me a cup of water? Thanks, I needed that. Now, maybe I'll live at least."

Then I noticed we were drawing a crowd, and there were boats all around us with some of them too close. Obviously, they had spotted this big fish jumping, but if they ran over our line, it could be cut in two. *Just keep working*, I thought. Eventually with a lot of "yanking and cranking," the fish was straight down, and the Dacron was back on the spool.

However, Captain Jerry reminded us that we still had over three hundred yards out. For some reason, I didn't find that overly comforting. Bud brought me another cup of water. My mouth was dry again, but I had the correct pumping technique going now, and even though it was tiring, there was no doubt in my mind that we were going to get this big fish. She was starting to come up. I looked at my watch and noted we had been on the fish for thirty-five minutes. First, we saw deep color, and then she was on the surface about twenty yards out. John had on the gloves, and the tag stick was rigged and ready. Bud was shooting pictures as fast as he could as the big fish was still trying to jump near the boat.

When we got the swivel to the rod tip, John wrapped the leader around his gloved hand, and Jerry came down from the bridge and tagged the fish. With a tape, he measured the length and width of the fish the best he could with the fish still in the water, and the calculated weight was over three hundred pounds. Not as big as we thought, but a nice-sized blue marlin. I'm not sure the calculation was accurate because of the length of the fish, it was very long. Sure fought hard and jumped high. We had achieved our goal. Jerry removed the lure and resuscitated the fish which we released but then, we had to retrieve the fish that was floating on the surface and resuscitate it again. It took three times before the fish could swim away. The fight had lasted fifty minutes, and my arms were quivering. She had put up a great fight. We cheered when she finally swam away, tired but okay, not even a drop of blood. She'll live to fight another day, and hopefully, the next angler that gets her to the boat will let her go again. They are too beautiful to kill.

Our next fishing day was not as successful. A mahimahi took one of the acoustical lures, jumped four times, and was off. Though we covered a lot of ground during the rest of the day, that was it. We had fished two days, had two strikes, but the result was great, one big blue marlin, which was better than most of the fleet. During the two days we fished, there might have been a couple of other marlins caught, but we were satisfied that our lures, our crew, and our luck, all made our trip a memorable one. We'll never forget it, that's for sure. I keep a photo of this big fish on my desk and I never get tired looking at it.

Fishing Kona, as always, had been a pleasurable experience for us, and we hope you'll give it a try someday.

Blue marlin
caught and
soon to be
released.

Fighting
fish—Jim
fighting
the blue
marlin.

Charlie Hall
with his
big bass.

Charlie and Jim
having fun
inshore fishing.

SWIMMING FOR OUR LIVES—AGAIN!
By Charlie Hall

———

"Charlie's story is partially tongue-in-cheek and a fun read, tried to kill me really!"

—Jim

I N MARCH OF 2016, I went down to southeastern Georgia to visit my classmate, old friend, and fishing buddy, Jim Paulk, on what had become an almost annual pilgrimage. I arrived on a Saturday and was glad to see Pat and Jim were aging like me but hanging tough to mobility and activity. Jim, through one of his farming buddies, had been given access to a private pond a few years before this visit. Jim and I had fished this pond many times before and caught some very nice fish. Jim and I had each caught largemouth bass over nine pounds in previous years and Jim had caught several fish that weighed more than five pounds. So, we knew well that the pond held some very nice fish. We were hoping to beat our existing records this year.

Before I arrived, Jim had acquired a new boat that was a little larger and even fancier than the one we used in previous years. The boat was designed for comfortable fishing, with seats that sat on pedestals about a foot tall. The boat was light and easily maneuverable with the trolling motor that Jim ran from the stern seat. All our trips were, at least in part, shakedown cruises for the new boat as every new mobile acquisition, on land or sea, requires some getting used to.

And so, we were in the process of learning about the boat and how it was handled, as well as fishing for some potential trophy bass. We fished on Saturday afternoon, twice on Sunday, and were out Monday afternoon, still searching for some bass—not only large in mouth but also in size. Saturday and Sunday brought us some fish but nothing of any size, mostly small ones in the one-to-two-pound range. Monday rolled around and the day was windy from the start. We chose to sit around the house and visit while we waited to see what the day's weather would bring. Around 3:00 p.m., the wind began to die down some, and we decided to give the pond a try. And so, we loaded up Jim's Jeep, and off we went in search of the monsters we hoped to find.

When we reached the pond, the wind was still not as quiet as we would have liked it, but there was a "lee" on the far side, and it appeared that we had fishing opportunities near the bass beds that we had seen on earlier trips. For those that do not know, bass beds are places in shallow water on the bottom, where the fish have swept away the vegetation and debris with their tails so what's left is a shallow depression where the females can lay their eggs and the males can come in and deposit their sperm to fertilize. Of course, every other species thinks of the eggs as dinner, and so, the males, and sometimes the females as well, will stand guard to keep invaders away. Bass beds are prime fishing spots during the spring when procreation is underway, so, we headed off across the pond with hope in our hearts and aggression in our souls.

We fished up and down the far bank, working our baits over the beds and the nearby places that looked like places we would be if we were bass. We were using plastic worms that are Jim's preferred lure for this pond, especially at this time of year.

The water temperature was not yet as warm as it would be later in the year and the cooler water tends to make the fish a little sluggish. We cast and cast, getting some bites and bringing a few fish to the boat, never even thinking about using the net since the fish caught were way too small to need a net. We just pulled them in close to the boat, grabbed the line, and hoisted them aboard to remove the hook and send them on their way to grow up and come back in a few years to be our trophy catches. I recall giving each of them instructions to remember I had not hurt them and to eat well, grow large, and bite my hook a few years from now when she was a lot bigger. And so, that's the way the afternoon went until we decided to give up, surrender to the fish, and head for home.

Now a little information is needed here to set the stage properly. The place where the boat is launched and recovered is on the bank, and the water just offshore is very shallow. The boat needs to be driven fairly well up the beach if the first mate [*author:* that's me!] is to get ashore with dry feet to pull the boat up a bit so that the captain (that's Jim!) can debark gracefully. It helps if the weight in the boat is more to the stern than to the bow so the bow is angled up a bit to allow the boat to slide up the bank easily.

And so, I got out of my seat to move back to where Jim was sitting and running the motor. I was standing up—for which I lived to regret later. As we were moving toward the landing site and about twenty yards out, for some unknown reason, the boat lurched a bit and I lost my balance. At that point, physics took over.

Now, please step over here while I pontificate a bit about those physics. The boat afloat has three centers of interest to us now but not seriously considered at the start of this episode. The center of buoyancy is the centroid (central point, so to speak) of the mass of water displaced by the boat and its contents. The center of gravity is, for practical purposes, the point at which all the mass can be considered to be located. The metacentre is the point at which a vertical line above the center of buoyancy intersects the original vertical line above the center of gravity. The distance between the center of gravity and the metacentre is called the metacentric height. All that's important to remember for this discussion is metacentric height is a measure of stability, with large being better than small. When metacentric height changes when the boat's heeling gets too small, the boat tips over and does *not* right itself. Got it? [*author:* Charlie, of course, spent a couple of years as a professor at Annapolis during his Navy career, and he's still teaching us.]

When I stood up and moved aft, the boat's center of gravity was moved upward, thereby reducing the metacentric height and decreasing the boat's stability—meaning that the boat was more likely to tip under small forces. And that's what happened. Something caused the boat to lurch, and the lurch caused the boat to roll a bit and, since my own center of gravity was definitely higher than the side of the boat, over I went. I think I grabbed at Jim [*author*: He did grab me!] to try to steady myself before I fell in, but ended up dragging him off his seat. The boat rolled back the other way after my weight was gone and then rolled again in the direction I had gone over the side. That caught Jim way off balance and over he went. So, we were both in the water, the motor was running off-center a bit and the boat was going in circles. Oh, by the way, neither of us was wearing a floatation device, and there was nobody in the boat to throw out the floatation cushion.

I went in head first, like how scuba divers enter the water, and so I don't know how far down I went. I next recall working to get upright and get to the surface. I opened my eyes and saw the bottom of the boat directly over me. I had this flash of fear about the propeller hitting me and slicing me up. It was a new motor, and the blades were sharp, indeed! I somehow got away from the boat and struggled to the surface, thinking it took forever to get a breath of air. I looked off to the center of the pond for the boat, hoping Jim would pull me out or, at least, tow me to shore. But immediately I saw the boat was empty so I looked for Jim. Off to my left, I saw a nose and some sunglasses, and I hollered at him, starting toward him—not very agilely in my barn boots, jeans, and shirt. He got his head out of the water and started swimming motions so I looked for the boat. It was still running in circles and the wind was pushing it toward the shore where we expected to land.

I managed to swim a little toward the boat, and after a bit, I was able to grab hold of the railing. Then I looked for Jim and saw he was making some progress toward the boat as well. About that time, I felt the bottom as the wind had fortunately pushed us shoreward while we were flailing about trying to stay alive. Jim was behind me holding on to the railing, and as soon as I could stand up, I pushed the boat closer to the shore. When we were almost there, Jim was able to stand up and reached the tiller to shut off the motor. Then I could control the boat better and got it beached a little while Jim was able to crawl ashore by holding onto the boat and crawling forward. He got to the beach and, using an older overturned boat as a helper, got to his feet. I called for him to get to the car and start blowing the horn for help as I started moving toward the beach to get out of the water.

The eighteen-acre pond belongs to David Brazell and his family, and luckily, it was late afternoon and David was home from work. The horn soon brought him running down to where we were huffing and puffing, just glad to be out of the water. He took over and helped us to get ourselves together. He told us that he would take care of the boat, our gear, and everything and said that he would charge the battery so that we could fish again when we were ready and sent us on our way home. However, David also delivered a strong ruling saying that we had been fishing for the last time without wearing a floatation device. "WEARING," he said. Jim and I were easy to convince, and we swore an oath, more powerful than blood or pinky-swear. We swore on our wet clothes and soaked shoes that we would *never* venture aboard any boat without wearing a floatation device.

When we got back to Jim's house, we had to face Pat. We soon fessed up to our misadventure—even if we thought about making up some story to explain our wet clothes. Pat shook her head and collected our wet clothes to put them in the washer. I rinsed out my muddy barn boots and set them out in the garage to dry. A reasonable estimate was that I'd be able to wear them again by the Fourth of July!!

And so, us boys in our eighties managed to survive what was a very harrowing experience. I was both scared for myself and terrified for Jim—especially when I first saw him in the water, nothing but nose and sunglasses. Later, I was far less confident I could swim to the boat that was being driven away from me by the wind. Second-class endurance swimming at the Academy came to my rescue because I learned back then I could do a whole lot more even after I thought I was exhausted. We did make it to shore, and I have no idea how long the whole thing took, but it was a really bad time for me until we were out of the water.

All is well now, and we fished again on Tuesday, when Jim caught a very fine fish, about five and a half pounds.

Jim with his big bass.

BIG BASS

———

A STORY WITH A BIG TITLE must be a special one—and this *is* a special one. After we moved to Georgia, near my younger brother Bobby, my farming blood started to boil, I simply had to get into farming. Since so many of my ancestors were farmers, it was a likely advocation for me in retirement.

First, I was introduced to Coach Thomason (former football and baseball coach at the local high school) who was the leader of a group that farmed in a community plot of land. He assigned me eight rows, sixty feet long. Coach and all the guys farming there told me where to order my seeds and helped me in so many ways, I was working in the dirt for sure.

When I arrived at Old Still Road, where our community garden was located, my friends always came to my plot to help. Watering vegetables by hand with a hose connected to the tap in my area was the acceptable way of keeping the proper moisture level on them. Time-consuming, but an efficient way of getting all water on your plantings instead of a lot of weeds.

Later, when I got into a conversation with a member of the

landscaping crew working in our neighborhood, Chris Brazell told me that his family farm of about five acres was not in use now, but maybe we could get his dad to plow a few rows for us. This plot of land had lain fallow (not used) for seven years. When we approached his dad, David, he decided to till the entire farm again, and while he was at work as a mechanic at JEA in Jacksonville, I was hoeing: thirty-two-rows planted, 432-feet long. Now, that's a farm! We had corn, squash, zucchini, watermelon, onions, potatoes, and finally a row of sunflowers to attract the bees to pollinate our crops.

Back in the old days, farmers depended upon regular intervals of rain for their crops, but nowadays if a source of water is nearby, like David has with a pond adjacent to his property, a set of rain birds with a pump was all that was needed to keep the crops going between rain showers.

With the sprinklers set at five feet high for maximum coverage, it was a beautiful sight to see them spraying outward and watering our crops. For me, this was like heaven. A pond of this size, about eighteen acres, must have fish in it too, I could almost smell them!

David, who became another son to me over the years, agreed to let me fish in the pond, which meant that I would need a small trolling motor for the ten-foot boat pulled up on the bank. Though I had done some largemouth bass fishing over the years, this was a chance to get into it more seriously. I would need not only the trolling motor and the proper fishing gear but more importantly, training. I needed someone to teach me how to catch bass every time I went out on the pond.

However, there was no one there to teach me. Fishermen in coastal Georgia are into fishing the saltwater creeks and rivers for speckled seatrout and redfish mostly. David's son, Chris, was a big help in getting me started because he had fished the pond since he was a little boy. The rest I had to learn on my own by reading everything I could find or watching videos of the pros catching bass.

Eventually, I found a way that worked for me: wacky rigged plastic worms. This is a crazy-sounding technique, I know—but after reading about it, I tried it, and it worked. The plastic worm was not breaking in half very often, and I was able to set the hook better.

Here's what I did: Using Senko five-inch plastic worms with a small rubber O-ring placed tightly around them, I put the hook under the ring to avoid cutting into the worm. If we put the hook directly into the plastic worm, it would often break in half during the fight. With wacky style, I could fish for hours without losing a plastic worm.

Then there was color. What to use? My favorite became Junebug—purple with emerald flecks. In fact, purple worms in any configuration seemed to work best in this pond. For me, that color gave me the most confidence. However, when two of us fished together, I always suggested that we use different colors to see which worked best that day.

Within a few years, we were having so much trouble patching a leak in the inner hull of the old boat, we replaced it with an eleven-foot boat that was very similar to David's. David, at one point, started calling me Captain Jim because it seemed to him as though everyone I took fishing caught bass. Some had never caught bass before, and I enjoyed sharing this freshwater bass-fishing experience with so many people. It was catch and release, of course, we never kept anything.

A Naval Academy classmate and great fishing buddy, Charlie Hall, came down from West Virginia for a week every year, and like me, he had a passion for fishing. Growing up in Mobile, Alabama, Charlie began fishing at an early age and became very good at it.

On a good day, we could catch and release twenty-five to thirty bass in the morning during a four-hour pond trip, and then go home and have lunch before going back for a few hours in the afternoon. We fished hard.

After fishing this pond so much, I had learned about many

spots that often held fish, so I could tell my fishing partner where to cast his bait. Charlie knew the spots too, and caught more than his fair share. We had lots of fun together, but the special day below is a day worth remembering . . .

After loading the boat and installing the trolling motor, we pushed the boat off the bank and left the area. There was a small dock only a few yards away, and we started casting around it, but nothing seemed to like our bait or its presentation. Since it was a nice calm day—with no wind—we would be able to fish the entire pond, not just areas out of the wind, making our day even more delightful.

We worked our way down the shoreline, Charlie was on the bow pedestal seat, and I was on the rear one. Charlie started off the day with the first fish—a nice one—he pulled out of some reeds, a regular spot for us. The fish was quickly put back in the water. As we worked our way around the pond, casting in our regular secret spots, we caught and released a few more fish. However, overall, we weren't catching as many as we expected.

Fishermen are fidgety, never satisfied with a bait unless they are catching lots of fish with it—and I'm the same way. I said, "Charlie, I'm going to switch over to a baby-bass-colored jerk bait to see what I can do with it." By now, we were on the far side of the pond with lots of structure along the banks and nothing happening.

Then, with a cast at a large dead limb that had fallen into the pond, I hooked up a big fish that ripped off quite a bit of my line. Knowing there were many snags along the shoreline, I moved the boat out and away from danger, leading the bass from the bank as well.

When she jumped, Charlie and I were breathless—she was huge! I believe we could've gotten an entire fist into her mouth. I just had to catch this fish! She took off again, stripping line off the reel and jumping twice, scaring me even though I was holding the rod down to stop her from jumping and throwing the bait back at me.

The reason that I'm saying "she," is because most males don't get over five pounds, and this fish had to have been double that. After the aerial display, she went to the bottom, and I couldn't move her. At the time, I thought she might be under a stray limb, so I tried every trick I could think of to get her started up.

Using only a six-pound test mono line, I had to be very careful not to break it. I put the reel into a free spool with a slackline to make the fish feel free and swim out from cover. That didn't work, and I started getting very worried we might lose her.

I moved the boat and pulled from three different directions, but nothing worked. I couldn't move her. Most of the time, bass fishing was about getting the fish to bite and setting the hook. The "yanking and cranking" part was a short, easy fight. But this was an epic fight over a long period of time, it seemed like forever!

This big fish had to have been big because she knew what to do to get free, she was a seasoned veteran. I told Charlie, "I'm going to get directly over her, clamp down on the drag, and pull as hard as I can. I may break the line, but I don't know what else to do." Suddenly, she started up, I couldn't believe it, "Charlie, she's coming up! Get the net." We were on the verge of catching a huge bass.

When she came into view, I instinctively reached down, got her by the lip, and pulled her into the boat. She was covered with grass from the bottom of the pond where she had been hiding. I peeled the chunk of grass from her as Charlie said, "You didn't even let me net her!" I apologized to Charlie, but I wasn't thinking.

After all the maneuvering around, this fish was *not* getting loose. We weighed her at nine pounds, ten ounces—my largest ever—and after taking photos, we watched her swim away. Our photo of this beautiful fish and watching her swim away made this one of our best bass trips ever. There's nothing like a very successful fishing trip for me.

George Perry
with Georgia
Game and Fish
official, Joe
Sterns, at the
Airpark.

Jim, otherwise
referred to as
"Frogskin" by
George Perry.

REMEMBERIN' GEORGE PERRY
(This story can originally be found in Georgia Backroads *magazine.)*

———

W HEN WE THINK of famous Georgians, among those who
come to mind are Jackie Robinson, Martin Luther King,
Bobby Jones, Ty Cobb, President Jimmy Carter, and Doc Holliday.
There are many others, but consider George Washington Perry?
What is his claim to fame? Well, if you are among the millions of
freshwater largemouth bass fishermen, you'll likely know his
name.

Like Babe Ruth, Bobby Jones, and Jim Thorpe, George Perry is
legendary in the sporting world, and while his mark was set
nearly ninety years ago, it is still in the record books. What did he
do? He set the standard every bass fisherman has dreamed of
duplicating or eclipsing. He hooked and landed the all-tackle
largemouth bass world record of twenty-two pounds, four ounces
on June 2, 1932.

The record was tied by Japanese angler Manabu Kurita, who
caught a twenty-two-pound, five-ounce bass in his country's Lake
Biwa in 2009. International Game Fish Association rules stipulate

world record fish under twenty-five pounds must break the preceding mark by two ounces. Los Angeles motorcycle policeman Bob Crupi caught a twenty-two-pound, two-ounce bass in California's Lake Casitas in 1990—close, but no cigar.

It was a long time ago, likely in the early 1970s, that I started hearing references to a record bass caught by a man named George Perry, but it was soon discounted. There was no way that it could have been the same George Perry that I knew in my hometown of Brunswick, Georgia, after World War II.

I was about thirteen, too young to drive, but old enough to get into all manner of mischief. I hate to mention it, but I was in trouble all the time—not serious stuff, but the adults back then didn't give kids a lot of slack.

We lived a few blocks away from a saltwater creek in Howard Coffin Park, not far from the Brunswick River. It was a creek with marsh grass and marsh hens, mud banks, ducks, and all kinds of things that were of interest to little boys. And we had lots of boys in my neighborhood. We were in and around the creek year-round when we were not playing ball of some sort.

After the war, our "private" swimming hole was "invaded" by a developer. A structure was going up in the very spot we used as a launching point for our activities. When the building was completed, we called it a marina. In fact, it was a small boathouse with an outside hoist to launch small boats into the creek. A small dock floated adjacent to it. This was not a major enterprise. To us though, it offered all kinds of possibilities.

The owner of our new playground was George Perry—hereafter called Mr. Perry because that was what we called him. He called us "frog skins," as in, "You frog skins, get outta here!" But boys don't know anything about "getting out of there." We were there all the time and learned to care for him in our own ways. Most adults had very little tolerance for us, perhaps rightly so.

He answered our millions of questions, tolerated us, and watched us with great interest. Or was it with concern? He had a warm smile, a twinkle in his eyes, and may have been a man who was a lot like us: full of the devil. He could kid around with the best of them, and what I would like everyone to know is if you met him, you'd never forget him. He was a true character, not just a name in a record book, and that is the principal reason why I want people to know about him.

One day, we were hanging around when a pickup truck towing a boat trailer pulled up to the marina. On that trailer was one of the strangest looking boats we had ever seen. It was a flat-bottomed, wooden rowboat with a five-hp kicker mounted on the transom. But what made the boat look so weird to us was that it had a canvas cover (like a Bimini top) supported by a lead pipe frame. It even had fringe hanging down from the canopy.

Mr. Perry looked at this most impractical craft, said nothing, and proceeded to lift it up and put it in the water. The four men who accompanied the boat were dressed in business suits and ties. One ran the boat next to the dock so that the other three could climb aboard. They were off for a cruise in their new "yacht." Climbing aboard was awkward because of the canvas top, two were able to crawl in. The fourth man, however, was having trouble. When he tried to climb aboard, he grabbed the pipe supporting the cover, stepped on the gunwale, and the boat promptly turned over. All aboard were dumped into the creek. To us kids, it was the funniest thing we'd ever seen. We laughed as the men pulled themselves out of the water. I looked at Mr. Perry, and he tried to hide it, but he had a grin on his face too. Definitely his kind of fun.

On another trip down to the marina, I noticed Mr. Perry was building a boat and had installed an automobile engine. That didn't look right to me. Car engines couldn't be put in boats, could they? Mr. Perry had the skills, faith, and (perhaps most important-ly) confidence to succeed. He finished the boat, got it running, and to my surprise, sold it. He also built speedboat runabouts from kits and sold them too. Then, the Coast and Geodetic Survey group recognized Mr. Perry's versatile skills and paid him to build a boat. He designed a boat that could be run up on sandbars, an unusual design for a boat in those days.

On another occasion, we ran down to the marina after school to see what kind of trouble we could get into. To our surprise, there was a beautiful mahogany speedboat far up in the marsh grass. It remained there for several days before it could be pulled out. We eventually learned what happened.

Talk about photo ops! The speedboat factory wanted to do a special promotion for a Fourth of July celebration, and the photographer needed the boat to be just at the right angle. This boat was known for its speed and was to head straight for the photographer, who was positioned in another boat with Mr. Perry.

The speedboat was to turn away at the last second, providing the needed shot. But it never made that crucial turn, and plowed into the photographer's boat, almost splitting it in two before running far up into the marsh. Mr. Perry jumped overboard to escape the collision, but his elbow was struck, and that arm was in a sling for a while.

Meanwhile, his oldest daughter, Barbara (nicknamed "Baby Doll") broke her arm in a playground accident at about the same time, leading friends to believe both had been involved in an automobile accident. Us kids kept a close eye on that marina from then on because strange and interesting things kept happening there.

What you are about to read has been told many times, but a good fish story bears repeating. Mr. Perry was a lad of nineteen, the oldest of five children living on a farm miles off the main road between McRae and Jacksonville, Georgia. His father had died a year earlier and putting food on the table in the depths of the Great Depression was a full-time, difficult job. A heavy rain made the fields too wet to plow, so Mr. Perry decided to go fishing. There was a full-fledged storm raging when he met his friend, Jack Page, owner of a pickup truck in which they made the twenty-mile trip to their fishing hole.

Mr. Perry had built a boat from scrap lumber that cost him seventy-five cents and had whittled a paddle from a piece of leftover wood. His friend hauled the boat down to Lake Montgomery in his pickup truck and, after launching, the boat was pulled up on the bank and kept there.

Lake Montgomery was an oxbow of the Ocmulgee River, formed many years before when the river changed course. There was an outlet into the river and during periods of high water, the lake would be "restocked" with various species of fish, including largemouth bass. At the time of the fishing trip, the lake was about a mile long, four hundred yards at its widest point. Many of the cypress knees lined the shore and dotted the shallow water. Mr. Perry fished the lake often, probably when his family needed food. Catching a few fish, or shooting a deer or some squirrels or doves was the principal source of food for the family. Sometime after the catch, someone asked him why he didn't freeze the fish and have it mounted. He laughed and said, "We lived so far back in the country we didn't have electricity for a freezer!"

When Mr. Perry and his friend arrived at the lake, weather hadn't improved, but they went fishing because they needed something to eat. During an interview years later, he said that conditions could not have been worse. High winds made it hard for him to control his casts.

He and Mr. Page took turns paddling and had no luck until, just before they decided to head home, Mr. Perry caught a small bass. Encouraged, they decided to keep trying. Out of the corner of his eye, Mr. Perry caught an interesting swirl, not a big one, but enough to take a shot at. He quickly cast his lure to the spot. The Creek Chub Fin Tail Shiner (in yellow perch scale) hit the water.

He had just the one rod and lure, so they were out of business if he lost it. And he didn't have enough money to replace it. He let it sink, gave it a twitch, and started reeling it in. Then the lure stopped. He feared it had snagged on an underwater cypress log, but the snag started moving. Mr. Perry reared back, set the hook, and the fight was on.

The fish jumped, and the two men shouted in astonishment at this "Queen of the Pond." After ten or fifteen minutes, Mr. Perry pulled the bass close to the boat, reached down and grabbed its mouth, and hauled her into the boat. His son, George L. (Dazy) Perry, told me much later that his father was too poor to own a landing net.

With this big fish in the boat, it was a good time to get out of the weather. Later they learned that a tornado had come down the river valley and totaled the Rock Hill Methodist Episcopal Church, just a few miles from their fishing spot.

On the way home, they stopped at Hall's Grocery in Helena to show off the fish. Mr. Perry's friends at the store told him about the *Field & Stream* magazine's Big Fish Contest and urged him to enter his catch for a chance to win seventy-five dollars in prizes.

The fish had to be weighed on certified scales and its girth and length measured. Helena's US Post Office was just across the street. The postmaster was Mr. Perry's friend and was happy to oblige. The fish was thirty-two and a half inches in length, twenty-eight and a half inches in girth and officially weighed twenty-two pounds, four ounces. Mr. Perry filled out the contest entry blank and mailed it in.

Mr. Perry took the fish home and cleaned it. It was a big female and had not spawned, so it was loaded with roe. His younger sister recalled years later, "It squirted all over the place." His mother fried it and served it to the family. It lasted for two days and Mr. Page likely was given his share too.

Sometime later, the *Field & Stream* package arrived and included a new rod and reel, a tackle box, a shotgun, and outdoor clothes. Later, Mr. Perry fished the Altamaha River backwaters, caught a thirteen-pound, fourteen-ounce bass, and won the *Field & Stream* contest, becoming the only entrant to win twice.

In the 1930s, Mr. Perry restored a World War I Harley-Davidson motorcycle with a sidecar. He courted his future wife, Pauline, on the machine, and I can visualize the couple traveling to "picture shows" in a nearby theatre. They wed in 1935.

Prior to World War II, Mr. Perry moved to Brunswick, about one hundred miles east of the McRae area. The coastal town at the time numbered about fifteen thousand people. He took a job at the Brunswick Pulp & Paper Co.—one of the two major employers in town. The pulp mill was on the south side and the Hercules Powder Co., was on the north side. Depending on which way the wind blew, you'd smell one or the other, and the odors were unpleasant. Few complained, however, because they provided jobs, and everyone had friends or family employed at one or the other. Wages were considered good at the time—twenty to twenty-five dollars a week.

When the war began, a small shipyard on the Brunswick River added six new ways to accommodate the construction of Liberty Ships to move war supplies around the world. People from all over came to Brunswick for work. To me, it seemed as though "war apartments" were built on every vacant lot in town to house the shipyard workers. The city population jumped to seventy-five thousand seemingly overnight. Schools went to two sessions a day and traffic on our little street was unbelievable. Wages and the opportunity to learn a new trade were available for many formerly destitute people—mostly farmers. Mr. Perry went to work there as a crane operator, later surviving an accidental fire that considerably frightened him. He said that dying in a fire must be the worst way to go.

By working seven days a week at the shipyard, employees made one hundred dollars per week, four or five times what they made prior to the war. Husbands and wives both worked there. Mr. Perry and many others were able to save sums used to establish new post-war businesses. After the war, the shipyard closed, and Brunswick seemed to become a ghost town overnight. It didn't, of course, because many workers stayed to help build a new city. Schools went back to one session, and provisions like sugar, meat, and gasoline became available again. Most importantly, the men came home from overseas.

Besides the marina, Mr. Perry opened a live bait business for a short time. He netted live shrimp and sold them to fishermen after the spotted trout and other fish in the tidal creeks and rivers around Brunswick.

His real talent was working as a mechanic. He only had an eighth-grade education but decided to study to become an airplane mechanic. He took courses and became a licensed airframe and engine mechanic. It wasn't long before he had earned his private pilot's license and was practicing takeoffs and landings nearby on Cumberland Island's long, straight beaches. In 1965, Mr. Perry took over a one-runway Airpark in Brunswick.

One example of Mr. Perry's mechanical ability came when a man who stopped by the Airpark one day and complained that his expensive car was running rough. So, Mr. Perry lifted the car's hood and quickly pulled all the spark plug wires out of the distributor cap. The owner was livid because he didn't think Mr. Perry could put those sixteen wires back in the right order. After doing so, the man started the motor, and it ran like a clock. Mr. Perry didn't have any testing equipment or maintenance manuals. He just had an incredible ability to make things work.

His son, Dazy, remembers watching his dad chase an FAA inspector out of the hanger while holding a wrench. Mr. Perry didn't like anyone interfering with his business although he enjoyed seeing visitors having a good time. He was a leader of a group of twelve to fifteen pilots who flew simulated dogfights over the marshes to the delight of us who watched.

About 1956, I had a chance to fly with Mr. Perry. My mother was ill and could not drive me to Savannah to catch my flight back to Annapolis. I called the Airpark and Mr. Perry said, "Come over, Jimmie, I'll fly you up." I don't remember anything about the flight because it was noisy, but I do remember that he taxied me right up to the back door of the terminal. I kept expecting him to stop the plane, but he kept going and going. When I got out with my B-4 bag and walked in the terminal door in my Midshipman's uniform, all eyes were on me. I'll never forget that magical moment Mr. Perry created for me. I looked back to wave goodbye, and there was that smile with a twinkle in his eye. It was special.

About those nicknames: he called his wife, "Honey Bunch";

youngest daughter, Celina, "Swootzie"; sisters Rubye "Rugby" and Cynthia "Sis"; the family physician, William F. Austin, "Dr. Mooney" (because that was the type of plane the good doctor flew). He called his dog, "Block," because all dogs were "Blockheads"; and, of course, us kids were "Frog Skins."

When I spoke with Dazy about the big fish and his dad, I asked if his dad ever talked about the fish or the record. Dazy said his dad never spoke at seminars about the fish unless he was being interviewed. But Mr. Perry loved to fish and sometimes paddled a canoe into the backwaters of the Altamaha River. He'd also fish for "winter trout" in the creeks. Many people wanted to fish with him because of his expertise.

I spoke with Terry Foreman, senior biologist and largemouth bass specialist with the California Department of Fish and Game, about the growth of bass. I had incorrectly assumed a big fish had to be an "old fish." However, he indicated that while age was a factor, genes were more important. Some fish get big, just as some humans get big.

What would be Mr. Perry's thoughts about the millions of fishermen hoping to break his world record? Dazy thinks his dad would be laughing it up and encouraging everyone to go for it. However, he would find it hard to believe that today's bass fisherman would spend so much money on a boat with a depth finder and other electronics, a powerful outboard motor, multiple rods and reels, electric motors, and other equipment. All he needed was a leaky, homemade, flat-bottomed boat, a paddle, one rod and reel, and a single lure. Of course, he had fisherman's luck.

Another thing Mr. Perry would be proud of, perhaps more proud of than the record was his son's personal record. He taught Dazy to fly at age twelve, and Dazy was a licensed pilot by the time he turned sixteen. He was hired by Delta Air Lines at age twenty, promoted to captain at age twenty-seven, and eventually retired from Delta as its number one pilot—or, as Dazy likes to put it, "Numero Ono."

George W. Perry died in a plane crash near Birmingham, Alabama, while delivering a plane in 1974.

BAJA FISHING ADVENTURE

———

A YEAR BEFORE WE EMBARKED on a long voyage in a twenty-six-foot trailer boat, my friend and fishing buddy, Bill Woodard, approached me with an idea for a fishing adventure: "Let's take my boat to Cabo San Lucas by water. With careful planning, we can have fun—fish every day and end up in a different anchorage at night instead of going home."

Planning, that's the keyword. Taking a trailer boat a thousand miles to Cabo by water requires a lot of careful planning. Boat size determines not only fuel capacity, but crew size, and the room available for everything from a spare anchor to spare oil. For a fishing trip lasting over three weeks, planning is the most important part of the trip. Supplies would be available once we got to Cabo, but on the way—except for a couple of fuel locations—nothing would be available for a thousand miles.

Bill's boat was a twenty-six-foot Blackman Fish Machine, equipped with a single 165-horsepower diesel engine, an out-drive, and a single 150-gallon fuel tank. A trip of this length on the open seas could be a dangerous experience, even for a big boat.

So why risk the trip? Lots of anglers enjoy trailering down to access good fishing areas at many launching ramps found along the Baja California peninsula. However, going by water was an adventure and gave us a chance to fish locations inaccessible to other trailered boats.

We began planning our trip about a year in advance by making a thirty-page checklist. Bill Woodard, the owner of the boat named *Fish-N-Fun*, was a veteran Baja California boater. He had made two previous trips to the Cape on a twenty-three-foot boat, with one of the trips ending in San Felipe on the Sea of Cortez. He was the key planner with the necessary experience for our expedition.

One of our many friends from our fishing club put us in touch with a similar Blackman boat, the *Katie M*, owned by Bill Holmes of San Diego. We arranged to meet Bill at Catalina Island one weekend to get to know him and his friend, John Nulton, first but, more importantly, to facilitate our spare parts inventory for each boat and to discuss details for our trip.

Each boat took a share of the spares, but each was responsible for everything else they would need. We gave them the thirty-page list that we had developed for everything we had to accomplish before the trip and items to store on the boat.

John Nulton, a retired San Diego police captain, was with Bill Holmes, a San Diego police detective. Bill's boat was powered with a two hundred HP diesel and had a portable gas generator. We agreed to rent a single-sideband radio for *Fish-N-Fun*, and both boats would install a GPS.

When we noticed that the San Diego boat had a "plow anchor," we suggested that a "Danforth type" would be more reliable in the various bottoms which we might encounter on the long trip. Later, they regretted not taking our advice. Except for an anchor alarm in the GPS awakening them as they slept nearby on the bridge, they might have gone on the rocks because their anchor was dragging.

We arranged with Mike Bales, author of *Launch Ramps of Baja*, to bring us and the boat back to Huntington Beach on Bill

Woodard's trailer. Bill Holmes made similar arrangements with Steve Blackman of Blackman Boats.

When we broke down this trip into successive daily legs, it didn't seem that complicated. Each day would be like cruising to San Clemente Island, fishing all day, and then going to an anchorage at night. The only difference was that we would end up in a different anchorage each evening with no store, no doctor, no mechanic, no fuel, and no water or electricity. We had to be self-sufficient!

At some anchorages along the Baja peninsula and offshore islands, we knew the local fishermen would come out to our boat to trade. Since the commercial fishing boats that supply them don't stop often, they'd be anxious to trade. So, we took a trade bag which included *Playboy* magazines, knives, transistor radios, many hats, heavy fishing line, hooks, and sorted items we didn't need any longer. We kept the bag on the bow bunks with other supplies. Since we had a long list of items stored in various locations on the boat, we also put on the list where items were stored to eliminate "Easter egg hunts."

On one evening, we anchored in the lee of an offshore island and noticed a plywood hut and a small panga on the beach upside down, with no people. However, after an hour or so, two men came out of the hut, got in the boat, and started heading our way. One man was rowing, the other was bailing. When they got to the boat, they had two large live lobsters. We gave them a couple of *Playboy* magazines, a bottle of wine, some fishing line, and ball caps. They were two happy fishermen as they rowed back to their hut, and as for the spiny lobsters? We put them in the live bait tank for a feast the next night. We also traded for shrimp one evening. Our trade bag paid off, and everything left over was given to the dock hands who were so helpful to us at the Cabo Marina.

We took on fuel at Turtle Bay, about 450 miles south of San Diego and our first fueling location, and later at Cabo San Lucas, which required a special technique called a Med moor. The piers at Turtle Bay were so high that none of the boats, even the big tuna seiners, could tie up alongside.

The procedure required dropping the anchor, backing in perpendicular to the pier, and casting two fifty-foot dock lines up to the dock for tying off where the lines would be crossed in the middle to keep the boat from moving. The fuel hose was then passed down to us and payment was made via a line and a bucket. We used a "Baja Box" filter system each of the three times that we refueled but found little sediment in the box. We could have gotten by without using it, but since the fuel is known to vary in quality, the consequences of not using a filter system make using one a requirement but it did slow down the fueling process.

Experience played an important role in our preparations. There were some great books available that detailed conditions at anchorages, reefs, and various fishing spots, and we kept them on the bridge and used them constantly—*Chart Guide, Charlie's Charts*, and *Launching Ramps of Baja.*

One of our key daily considerations was to arrive at our destination in time to anchor with daylight, and we stuck to this throughout the trip. We frequently left in darkness but navigating into a strange anchorage area in daylight made sense to us.

We left Huntington Beach on October 21 at dawn and filled the bait tank with small mackerel we caught at the fourteen-mile bank off Newport Beach. When we arrived at the San Diego Marlin Club that afternoon, the *Katie M* was already at the dock, and there was real excitement behind the smiles of Bill Holmes, a San Diego detective, and his former captain, John Nulton. Like us, they were anxious to get going.

We went to the fuel dock and emptied the fuel from our 150-gallon main tank into our three fifteen-gallon drums and two five-gallon containers that we kept under the ladder to the flying bridge as our emergency fuel stash. Each boat took a total of 205 gallons of diesel. When we used fuel out of the fifteen-gallon containers after transferring the diesel into the main tank, we disposed of them to make room in the cockpit where they were secured.

As we filled the tank for the first time in San Diego, we calibrated the fuel gauge so we knew exactly how many gallons we had in the tank, based on the reading on the gauge.

Afterward, we had dinner with the Blackman family who had built both boats, and made final arrangements to call Don Blackman on the satellite radio at 8:00 p.m. each night to let him know where we were so he could call our families to keep them posted on the progress of our trip. How many boat builders do you know that would do this for a customer? He was an important part of our trip and a great voice to hear every night.

At midnight, the wind died down, and we could wait no longer. We headed south at our calculated hull speed of 7.2 knots, our most fuel-efficient speed. For the next couple of weeks, we rarely varied from this speed. We ran all day and anchored at Colnett before dark. This was a bluff area, providing a lee from the normal northwest wind only. Dinner with the only two steaks we had aboard was great, the moon was full, and we went to bed full of excitement.

At midnight, we were awakened. The seas were coming from one direction and the wind another. Talk about misery! We were almost tossed out of our bunks! We tied a bridle on the anchor line and tied it off at the stern which moved the bow into the seas. This helped for a while, but we couldn't keep up with the changing conditions and decided to head south at 3:15 a.m. This was the only uncomfortable anchorage we encountered on the entire trip, a scary, rough night.

At daybreak, we had a nice rainstorm that washed off the boat a little. We were just off the west end of San Martin Island, and put the fishing lines into the water at 6:45 a.m. At 7:15, we went by a kelp paddy with three lines out. We took three yellowtail, all released at 7:45, and three thirty-pound yellowfin tuna, also released. Our final count was eleven tuna and seven yellowtails—and we were just transiting the area. Think what we could have done if we really fished there! *Katie M* did about the same. Later, we anchored at Jeronimo Island. It was windy, but the seas were calm thankfully.

Soon after, we got underway. Waiting for daylight was important because of the need to navigate through the lobster pots and the proximity of the dangerous Sacramento Reef where many boats had run aground in the past. Then the weather turned nasty on us, rain squalls, wind, and a rough following sea. We decided to head for Cedros Island at cruising speed to arrive in daylight and anchor at the north anchorage, which was the best one on the island. It sure felt good to get into a calm area after negotiating the infamous Cedros channel. We were now 357 miles from Huntington Beach. The *Katie M* side-tied with us for margaritas and dinner. Great time with new friends on a real adventure.

On October 25, we were up early, feeling as if we'd overdosed on sleep, but this had been a great anchorage. Our plan was now to fish the lee side of Cedros Island and end up in Turtle Bay to refuel. We caught some nice calico bass on plastics and light iron, and then, that afternoon, we took on one hundred gallons at the Turtle Bay Pier. This meant we arrived with fifty gallons in reserve.

As we were fueling, one of the passengers on a big yacht fueling next to us—who had purposely ignored us—finally condescended to speak to us on our "little" boat. They looked down at us and, thinking we launched the boat nearby, asked, "Where did you launch your boat?"

When we replied, "Huntington Beach," they had a hard time believing that we'd come all the way from there and were headed to the Cape in our "little" boat. That was one of the highlights of the trip, telling those snobs we were 450 miles from home, coming all the way on the water. We anchored off the end of the pier for the evening and took our first shower from a sun shower bag filled in San Diego—we even shaved.

On October 26, we left Turtle Bay at daybreak with a full load of fuel and some rust-colored ice, which we put in our ice chest.

The water temperature was 71.1°F and, for the first time in several days, we found the seas calm with just the normal Pacific swell to rock the boat a little. We released a skipjack tuna and, just before noon, *Katie M* caught the first wahoo of the trip on a marlin jig. Later, we caught a nice bull Dorado on a chrome wahoo jig, and at about 1:30 p.m., we pulled the lures and headed for Asuncion at cruising speed. Winds had increased to over twenty knots with quartering seas.

The Blackman handled the following seas well, and we were happy the weight of the extra fuel was low in the boat, adding to our stability. It's a good idea to put heavy items as low as possible in the boat, including getting one person off the bridge in rough seas. As we entered Asuncion Bay, we measured the wind speed at twenty-five to thirty, with gusts thirty-five mph, the wind was high in the anchorage, but there were no waves. The *Katie M* graciously shared their wahoo with us for dinner and, as you know, you can't beat wahoo, the best!

On the morning of October 27, we were very excited. Our next stop was Abreojos, an exciting place we'd read about. Abreojos in Spanish means "open your eyes or lookout," and for good reason—the entire area is covered with reefs and countless lobster traps. Larger boats did not dare go into this area, but our small boat was a distinct advantage for fishing there.

En route to Abreojos, the wind was blowing twenty to thirty mph, and we were anxious to get around Punta Abreojos, but gave it a wide berth to miss the outside reef and arrived at our destination in mid-afternoon. The fishing was incredible! The *Katie M* caught a five-pound calico bass on plastics on every cast! Our location wasn't quite *that* good, but it was still the best bass fishing we'd ever seen. We caught and released one eight-pound pinto bass (spotted cabrilla) on a six-pound test. What a fight!

On October 28, we fished Abreojos all day, catching and releasing bass on light tackle. Between the two boats, we caught and released pinto bass from five to fifteen pounds. Best fishing I ever experienced, mostly using pink plastic scampis—lots of them—the fish were chewing them up. Reluctantly, we left Abreojos after dinner, had a couple of hours of sleep, and picked our way around the lobster traps by using our hand-held spotlight. Needless to say, we went out slowly and cautiously, as I directed the way on the bow with the spotlight.

At daylight, we put the lures in and set our course for Thetis Bank, an incredible place to fish. The water temperature was now up to seventy-six degrees. However, a little after 7:00 a.m., we had our first scare of the trip: a squealing sound was coming from the engine compartment. This was one of those, *Oh, you know what!* Moments. When I went down to find the source of the noise, it was scary. No mechanics to call on the phone for help. We found the power steering oil reservoir empty. It had leaked out through a hole in the oil cooler and we didn't have a spare. We decided to make our own cooler with a spare hose. We bypassed the cooler With a long section of the hose, coiled it in a bucket of water, and replaced the fluid that had leaked out. Remember the movie, *Apollo 13*? That was us, making do with what we had—resourceful! It worked too.

This was our oil cooler for the balance of the trip. Each hour, we dumped the water into the bilge, filled the bucket with our wash down hose, and then pumped the bilge. This process took less than thirty seconds. We were thankful the problem turned out to be a manageable one. Both boats caught a wahoo and dorado on the bank and headed for the anchorage at Bahia Santa Maria inside Punta Lazaro—a nice spot to spend the night out of the wind.

For the next two days, we fished offshore and had many doubles on wahoo and dorado. The wahoo bite generally shut off around 9:00 a.m., but the biggest that we caught, about seventy pounds, hit a marlin jig at noon.

With no way to refrigerate fish, we released everything except one for dinner and kept the leftovers to mix with the powdered eggs for breakfast or to use in fish tacos. We were fishing for food, which was our plan from the beginning. The boat had a tiny freezer compartment that held two steaks when we left home, but afterward, we put water in a zip lock bag to make ice during the day while the engine was running. In the evening, while on the anchor, we broke up the ice for margaritas, listened to music, and refilled the bag. Great life on a little yacht!

On November 1, we went to San Carlos for fuel, a zig-zag trip inland of about one and a half hours while I spent time on the bow, looking for shallow water since we were told the navigation devices were not to be trusted. We were required to go through customs, immigration, and present our papers to the Captain of the Port in order to get a fuel permit. At least they had fuel. Sometimes they don't.

While the three guys were ashore (the two captains and one who spoke Spanish), I was alone to guard the two boats, tied up to the *Katy M* which was tied up to a large tuna boat at the dock. Suddenly, I started seeing lots of activity on the tuna boat, and I'm thinking they look like they are about to get underway with us tied to them. So, I thought I'd have to start up our boat with the *Katy M* tied to us and maneuver back to the dock to get tied up to it alone.

Miracle of miracles, with no communications with the crew on the tuna boat, they backed out and passed our lines to a man on the dock who tied us up as the tuna boat got out of the way. When the three got back to the boat and saw the tuna boat gone, I explained the drill I had gone through without help. That was a laugh, but I had been very concerned when that boat started backing out!

By 3:00 p.m., we were back at Punta Redonda where we caught yellowtail and barracuda on candy bar jigs. We gave the fish to the Mexicans trolling handlines from pangas, and they were happy to get them!

On November 2, we were up at 2:00 a.m., and since the weather looked good, we left on the longest leg of the journey—167 miles, for Cabo San Lucas, our goal.

As we trolled the high spots and ran at cruising speed in

between them, we caught and released a big striped marlin off Punta Tosca and released many dorados as well. The water temperature was now up to seventy-eight degrees Fahrenheit, and it was dark as we docked in the downtown Cabo Isles Marina. We were back in civilization again for the first time in almost two weeks.

The next morning, we turned over our paperwork to the Marina office, and they took care of everything for us—at a price of course, but it was worth it. Carl and Suzie Sandahl, the managers, did everything they could to make our stay a memorable one. The facilities were nice and secure (twenty-four-hour security patrol with card key gate) as any you'll find in a nice marina in the US.

Mike Bales joined us with the boat trailer, and the balance of *Katie M*'s crew joined them. Mike wrote a column in *Western Outdoor News* and wrote a book on *Trailer Boat Ramps in Baja*; he knew the roads well and had a big truck with an extra fuel tank in the back of it.

His long trip down was not without some drama. Some kids were playing along the side of the road and chased some cows onto it, but Mike saw them and managed to dodge them with the truck, but the trailer hit one. When he got out of the truck to check the damage, the kids were long gone, and the cow was dead.

The poor trailer was severely bent and incapable of holding a boat. Along the way, Mike found a welder to repair the trailer. When Mike arrived in Cabo, we had six days of great fishing with him as his reward for bringing the trailer down along with paying his expenses. Water temps at the Cape were over eighty degrees, and we caught marlin, sailfish, dorado, and tuna—you already know about Cabo fishing. It's great!

We tried refueling in Cabo in the morning while the "fleet" of charter boats was out, and at high tide. It was a hassle and dangerous because of broken pilings underwater we saw off the inside end of the pier. They could easily have punched a hole in the bottom of the boat. The dock attendants didn't warn us, and it was every man for himself to get to the dock. We had to be aggressive like the other boats, and thankfully, we only had to refuel one time. Remember those small mackerel we caught off Newport Beach? We released them in the marina before we hauled the boat out, never used one, and none died on that long trip—an amazing bait story.

On the day before we started home, we hauled the boat out and spent the night at a campground in the boat on the trailer. When we heard that a bad storm was coming, we wanted to get as far north as we could before the it arrived. So, after pumping the remaining diesel out of the boat tank and into the big tank in the back of the truck to relieve the weight on the trailer hitch, we started up the road.

The trip home was not without challenges, in fact, we had several. First, we came to a place where a landslide covered both lanes of the road, but with a little room on the side, we managed to barely get around the slide area and stopped at a small motel to spend the night. While we slept, it rained hard all night, but stopped by the time we left in the morning. However, when we got a few miles up the road, there was a river of water fifty yards wide, running over the road with a few vehicles backed up heading south.

Obviously, this was a very dangerous situation. We stopped and watched, but the flow of water never slowed. It was going to take a long time for the water to flow out of the mountains. Then, we held our breath and watched as a large motorhome heading south started through the raging water. When they made it through, Mike said, "We have a lot of weight with us, I believe we can make it through too." At that, we started through the torrent very slowly but soon gained enough confidence to go a little faster, and, hey, we made it. WHEW!

We only had one other incident when a Mexican driver in a small, closed-in truck we saw a lot in Baja, passed us from behind and—we believe deliberately—bumped our boat. We think he was trying to wreck us for salvage purposes, but it didn't work.

Mike was too good of a driver, with experience driving in Baja. Later, when we stopped and checked for damage, the boat had a spot of red paint from the truck, and his outside rearview mirror was in the boat. This had been a close call in a very remote area. Having never met Mike prior to this Baja trip, we became life-long friends.

We arrived home on November 15, at midnight. Total mileage from Cabo to Huntington Beach was 1,131 miles. It was a lot of work but traveling and catching fish with good friends made it worthwhile. Next time, we'd like to take two months instead of one. For us, that's the only way to make it better.

As an addendum: We asked an experienced emergency room doctor, Dr. Mike Thomas, what to carry onboard. His recommendations included prescription antibiotics, anesthetics, splints, first aid books, etc. Though we didn't use the medical bag, it was comforting to know we were ready should a need arise. This is something that should've been considered.

If you must use the life raft in a hurry, you may only have time to grab one item. What would that be? We had an "abandon ship bag," with everything we needed in one place. Well, maybe not everything, but hopefully enough to help us survive until rescuers could find us.

Here is a partial list of what we put in our bag: canned food and water, fishing gear, whistles, flares, a signal mirror, EPIRB, handheld VHF, and more. Again, we didn't have to use this bag, but we kept it where we could grab it in a hurry. Having an "abandon ship bag" could be important. We had fun, planned carefully, and stayed safe. We made it home alive.

A river
rushing
down the
mountains,
across the
road home
from Cabo.

Wahoo
given to
our
Japanese
friends
who we
met at
Thetis
Bank.

Haul out at the Cabo San Lucas Marina
by Mike Bales for the long trip home.

MY LOVE STORY

WHEN I MET Patricia Ann Metzler, I was definitely hit with an arrow in the heart. There are no words to express my initial reaction to the moment I met her; she had an aura about her that was so engaging, I knew she was the girl I wanted to marry.

As for previous relationships, I had the usual teenage romances—but none lasted. A funny one said: "I'm not waiting around four years for you to graduate from Annapolis, I'm going to Georgia to find me a husband." I've laughed about this remark all my life and shared it many times. I later heard that she had found four of them. Maybe I dodged a bullet, huh?

During my third-class year (sophomore) at Annapolis, a friend and classmate, Stan Dunlap, invited me to join him on a three-day weekend leave to Delaware. Since I had no binding relationship at the time, it sounded great to me. His then-girlfriend, Sheila Cunningham, set me up with three blind dates.

What I remember from that weekend was that Stan and I were made guests at the Sigma Nu Fraternity house and slept in bunk beds in a room with the windows open—freezing outside and inside. Extra blankets were needed for sure! We survived though.

I have no recollection of the first two blind dates, but number three—wow! I was stunned shortly after meeting Pat, because I had never met anyone like her. She was so enchanting, I knew immediately she was the girl I was going to marry. Our evening together was special. We seemed to be so comfortable together, as if we had known one another for a long time. She seemed to have a big heart and was so mature. I was deeply impressed.

When I learned that Pat had just broken off a relationship with the captain of the Delaware basketball team, and only agreed to the blind date as a favor to her friend, I knew she had no interest in starting a new relationship anytime soon. However, I was going to do my best to get her to come down to Annapolis for a formal dance.

As for military academies, she had gone up to West Point with a high school friend who was dating a cadet, and wasn't overly impressed, I guess. One thing about Pat was that she had carefully thought out her plans for her life, and living in a military marriage had no appeal to her. So, I had to call upon all my persuasive skills to get her to come down to Annapolis for a dance. At the time, I didn't know how much she loved to dance—which might have been the primary reason she ended up coming. I do remember many phone calls and letters were involved in the "getting her to come down" part.

On that special day, when I was to meet Pat on a Saturday in Annapolis, we had agreed to meet at a certain time on the front steps of Bancroft Hall, the largest dormitory in the world. She was there in a Delaware sweatshirt, thinking that she might not recognize me and I'd have to find her—very characteristic of Pat. Well, there she was, with a gorgeous smile on her face, the most beautiful girl I had ever dated. Having spent so little time together, there should have been an awkward moment, but there was none.

With her good looks and personality, she had dated a lot, but I later learned she didn't date anyone for very long. As previously mentioned, Pat had thought out her plans for life to include teaching elementary school and coaching kids after graduating from Delaware. If a guy she was dating didn't fit comfortably in those plans, she moved on.

Graduating from Annapolis was my greatest dream in life, and it was a rigorous and challenging experience for me with another two and a half years before I would graduate. Marriage was far from my mind, but I knew she had to be my wife someday—I didn't want to lose her. I'm not saying there was a magic moment when everything clicked, but we knew from the beginning that we liked each other. This was only the beginning of a sixty-two-year love story.

When I met Pat, I had no idea what a good athlete she was, but competitive? Just ask her granddaughters, who use to sit on the floor and play cards with her. While she talked with that beautiful smile on her face, they would tell you she had the heart of an athlete with a keen determination to win. She was into winning, though you would never know it. She was so nice, none of us wanted to recognize her determination to whip us. However, that same determination led her to take on and complete whatever she needed to do.

So, where did that competitive spirit come from? In high school, she was on the track team and did many events, including the long jump and several races. Many years later, when we lived in California, a high school classmate called from Pennsylvania to invite her to a class reunion, but she was at a meeting. At the conclusion of our conversation, he said to tell her that her high jump record was still good. Wow! I never knew she did the high jump. She played basketball too, but her favorite sport was swimming and diving. She loved the water and did water ballet at Delaware because the training for it allowed her adequate time for her studies.

When we try to analyze why Pat was so driven, in her own way, she had a huge heart and wanted to please others and win for her team. That was an inherited trait, but she learned how to enhance her ability to compete by training hard and was fortunate to train during her high school years at her local swimming club under one of the best swim coaches of all time, Peter Daland. Look him up. He won 9 NCAA Division 1 championships at Southern California and coached both the men's and women's Olympic swim teams to victory in different years. She learned what it took to win and how to face life with confidence from him.

By Pat's third visit to Annapolis, we knew we liked each other and thoroughly enjoyed being together. We wrote many letters and talked on the phone some even though access to a phone was limited because, at Annapolis, we had to share the phone with others wanting to use it.

After the class of 1955 graduated, our class of 1957 didn't go on summer leave. We were introduced to aircraft carrier life and flew in a plane taking off and landing. It was a propeller-driven airplane. What we called, "aviation summer" continued with a visit to Patuxent Air Base where we were introduced to experimental Naval aircraft and had our first flight in a jet engine plane. Then, after three weeks of playing and training as Marines, we made an assault on a beach in a landing craft. That completed our summer training before our leave began.

So, due to being on the carrier Valley Forge for three weeks and playing marine, I didn't see Pat for two months. A long, long time. But when training was over, I finally met Pat's parents who lived in Rose Valley, Pennsylvania, south of Philadelphia. They could not have been nicer or more welcoming. Naturally, I was nervous prior to meeting them, but very quickly, I was over that. I felt right at home there, and Pat and I had our first extended time together. No matter the setting, our love was blossoming.

Spending time at Pat's home, and then taking her down to Georgia to meet my family, cemented our relationship; we desperately wanted to be together. There was no doubt that I loved her with all my heart, and she felt the same about me. Being more mature at this point, we both were ready for a grown-up relationship, and at the beginning of second-class year, Pat agreed to wear our class crest pin, certifying that she was engaged to be engaged. We had shown our commitment to each other.

During my last two years at the Academy, I had two wonderful roommates, Warren Zimmer who was going into the Air Force after graduation, and Earl Piper who was going into the Marine Corps. Earl's dad was finishing up thirty years in the Corps, so, between his dad and an uncle who was a Marine general, I was under pressure to enter the Corps too.

In the fall, the Marine officers stationed at the Academy sponsored a dance for the midshipmen who were pledged to the Marines after graduation. It was a small affair, sixty-three midshipmen and their ladies. A local reporter was there and took photos of Pat and me with the leading Marine officers there. As it turned out, Pat and I were featured in the Annapolis newspaper, others saw the beauty in Pat too—it sure wasn't me.

Later that year, I decided I wanted to go into the Navy and get into Submarine School. And my classmates who were going in the Corps had a little shindig to present me two steel balls, symbolic of Captain Queeg in the movie, *The Caine Mutiny*. When he became nervous, he'd take the steel balls out of his pocket and grind them together. This was fun, and I enjoyed the camaraderie, and yep, I still have those balls. Earl made a career in the Corps and retired after thirty years as his dad had done.

Pat came down to Annapolis as frequently as she could, and on many of those occasions on Saturday afternoon, I was up in the green chair officiating varsity tennis matches, but I had no trouble finding a sixth company classmate to escort her around until my official duty was over. I played on the Plebe tennis team, but I had nowhere near enough talent to play on the varsity. The top players were completely out of my league. My claim to fame was that I won the brigade intermural tennis championship with my partner and classmate, Al Senior.

At the end of the third year in Annapolis, our second-class year, the big event was the Ring Dance, where we were going to dip our rings in water shipped to the Academy from the naval ships all over the seven seas, a tradition started in 1925. A committee had designed our Academy class rings to be unique ones, Pat's diamond engagement ring was picked out by my Uncle George Cunningham, and paid for out of my savings account where I deposited my paychecks over the years and many jobs. After the dance, we proudly wore our rings, and were finally, officially, engaged—as were many other classmates. Pat was gorgeous in her beautiful formal gown, and we danced to almost every song. She was an excellent dancer, light as a feather.

First-class year, our senior one, I oversaw things happening all the time. Here's an example of how to get demerits: I'm marching my company classmates back to Bancroft Hall when Captain Patton, the officer of the watch, detected two friends and classmates talking in the rear of the column. He reported me because I was in charge. He was the son of George Patton, the famous WWII general, and the captain was an exchange officer. In return, the Naval Academy had sent a Naval Officer to West Point for a year. The previous year, I had no demerits, but when someone didn't get out of their bunk on time, I was on report again.

The Captain Patton incident was an untimely one. I had to call Pat to tell her not to come down the next day for a formal dance in Memorial Hall, a special occasion. So, I'm at the dance in formal uniform, white gloves, and a sword, of course, as MOOW (Midshipman Officer of the Watch). As I was standing at the door as people were leaving, one of the officer's wives remarked, "Thank you, we had a wonderful time."

I replied, "I'm glad that you enjoyed the dance." However, I was thinking: "Boy, I sure didn't." On watch, no dance or Pat for me!

At our graduation ceremony, we tossed old hats in the air and put on new ones for photos around the yard (campus) with families, many of whom had never been there before. Roommate Earl Piper was now a Second Lieutenant in the Marine Corps, while my other roommate, Warren Zimmer, had his new Air Force uniform on. I had my Ensign Shoulder Boards on, and there was a mass exodus as classmates said their goodbyes and left Annapolis.

Some stayed for marriage ceremonies in the chapel, one every thirty minutes with brides literally dressing in a car. This was something that Pat—absolutely—did not want for her wedding experience.

We left for Pennsylvania, where we had the wedding rehearsal the same night as graduation at the Swarthmore Presbyterian Church, then dinner, and finally the bachelor party at the Media Inn. Most of us were not used to drinking so much and the alcohol did us in. They kept forcing me to have "one more drink" and though my brother, Bobby, tried to keep me sober, it was a losing cause. They put me in a corner of the room on the floor, which was okay for a little while, but I had the address for the house Pat's family had arranged for us to use that night. Not good if I was out cold.

They got me loaded in a car, and the caravan of cars set out to find our sleeping arrangements. One of my high school class-mates who graduated from West Point the previous year, Carl Croft, remembered the street name and started going up to back doors, trying them, until he found one unlocked. Inside an unlocked door, he found some mail on the table to verify the cor-rect name. Finally, the right house!

That night, the gods were with us. No one was shot for being in the wrong house, and everyone found a place to sleep: beds, couches, closets, the floor—anywhere they could find room. I have a faint recollection of the car ride and being carried into a bedroom. It's a good thing Pat didn't know what was happening to the man she was about to marry. You can guess our condition the next morning, half of us were throwing up and in very bad shape. If the wedding had been in the morning, I never would have made it.

Some of the guys didn't hang around for the two o'clock wed-ding but headed north to their homes. Meanwhile, the owners of the home arrived to find a bunch of sick guys. She said she knew exactly what to do to get us over our hangovers, and fixed us an appropriate breakfast. By noon, we were ready to prepare for the wedding. All four military services were represented, and no one was stabbed by a sword. That's a good thing!

The wedding went off without any problems, save for a little rain, but I had the most beautiful bride in the world. We were married at last! My love for her was unending, and I've been wondering for all the years that we were together how fortunate I was that I found her and she loved me.

As I write this, she has been gone for five years, and I still tell her I love her every day and get teary-eyed at the least memory. She lived her life to please others and succeeded in doing so.

The wedding reception was at the rustic Old Mill, where early Little Theater started. Her parents were very involved in Little Theater productions. Pat's dad graduated from Ohio State University and her mom from Toledo University, a Metzler and a Morton, about as German as you get. Pat had the most beautiful blue eyes and blond hair, of course. Our tiered wedding cake was cut with my sword and all the traditional things were done, but I was anxious to get out of there and head south for Treasure Island near Tampa, where we could have each other, full time, with no distractions, just letting our love for one another grow.

One of the stories she liked to talk about from our honeymoon experience demonstrated how caring and generous she was. It went like this: "Before he [Jim] got up, I went to the grocery store to buy everything needed to fix him a special breakfast in our motel on the beach. By the time he got up, breakfast was ready. I asked him if he knew how to put the leaf up on the little dinette table. He said 'Sure, we have one that works like that at home.'

"When I put his breakfast on the table, and he sat down to eat, the eggs went over one shoulder, and the orange juice went over my other one!" That leaf didn't snap into place and what was her reaction? "Let's clean this mess and start over again." She told this story many times over the years, and we learned early in our marriage how to deal with problems, large and small. We never argued and if we disagreed, we put it on the back burner until we had more facts. Pat came from a wonderful family and did her best to use that as a model for our family—I wasn't about to change anything either.

After spending a few days with my family when we returned from our honeymoon on Treasure Island, we left for Covington, Kentucky, to be at my roommate's wedding. On an old country road there, we saw a sign for the Renfro Valley Barn Dance. I told Pat, "If we go by here before it starts on Saturday night, we have to stop." After Warren Zimmer's wedding, which went great, we stopped to go to the Barn Dance. However, there was only one motel there, and it was full, of course. What were we to do? This rather large lady was sitting in a chair near the check-in desk, not by accident. "Honey, I have room at my place, we are off the old road."

So, we said, "We'll follow you over there."

After checking in, we went to our room to change, I had on dress white uniform, and Pat had on a silk dress. Walking into the room was like an 1890 movie, I kid you not. A bowl with a pitcher of water, and a flashlight to get to the outhouse in the dark. Being married to me, Pat was in for an adventure. The Barn Dance was fun, with good music and good folks.

When it was over, Pat said, "I have to go to the bathroom."

I said, "The flashlight is there."

Pat quickly came back to the room and exclaimed, "There are cows out in that field, I'm not going out there by myself!" So, I guarded my new wife to her first experience using an outhouse. My Pennsylvania girl was getting a good dose of the old south. She must have loved me a lot because she never complained. The next morning, we got dressed, left as fast as we could, and later checked into a nice, downtown Atlanta hotel. Quite a contrast. Back to the twentieth century!

A few days after visiting Atlanta, we were back in Brunswick, staying at my house when Bobby, my brother, suggested a fishing trip near Darien, only fifteen miles away. Fishing in the swamp area off the Altamaha River would be Pat's first experience in a swamp, a new adventure for her. Bobby went with the guide in one boat, while Pat and I were in a second boat.

In the swamp, we decided to go back, but finding our way out was challenging since we were so deep that we had to find an open channel to get out. However, when I tried to go in any direction, the brush closed in on us, forcing us to go a different way. Pat was getting a little anxious and wondered if her husband was going to find their way out of this thick swamp. About that time, she saw a snake swimming toward us, and when she pointed it out, I saw it swimming right on top of the water. I said, "It's a cottonmouth, maybe we can take him back with us." Before Pat could say anything, I whacked him hard with an oar, and Pat screamed.

And after this harrowing experience, Pat said, "Don't ever do that again! I was ready to jump out of the other side of the boat except I thought that there might be another one there." Of course, growing up in the woods and swamps, we did what came naturally to us, and Pat's life continued to adjust to this southern boy. She trusted me, and that was a good thing because living with me would be an adventure, as she was learning, one snake at a time.

We soon left Georgia to find Route 66 for our trip west to find a place to live and for me to report to my first duty station in San Diego aboard the USS Montrose APA 212. Neither of us had ever been west before, and everything we owned was in the '55 car that I received as a graduation present from my family. We had car troubles but managed them and decided to stop in Las Vegas. This was an exciting new world for us, our eyes were busy taking in the wonder of the new sights while we listened to new sounds. There was no Strip then, only downtown, and having heard of the Golden Nugget, we went there. It was full of people playing slot machines like the illegal ones at our golf course in Brunswick. It was excitement like we had never seen before.

We gravitated toward the craps table because everyone was shouting with non-stop action there. We had never seen anything like it. As we watched, a man gambling there, turned around and started talking to Pat, explaining the game to her. He felt she was bringing him luck and asked her to hold his silver dollars for him.

When it was his turn to roll the dice, he wasn't doing it fast enough because of his conversation with Pat. The croupier who was responsible to keep the game going became very upset, and the man was mad too—may have had a few drinks, but he threw the dice at the table and started to walk away. We said, "Wait, we have your money."

He said, "You keep it, I would lose it anyway, just don't gamble with it and get out of here."

When we got back to our room, we counted the silver dollars, and it was enough to pay for our room and dinner with a little leftover. We were happy about our good fortune but sorry for the man who gave it to us. From looking at his hands, he was likely a hard-working laborer who could ill afford to give money away. This was another real-life experience for us, we were so naïve, but Pat's charm was so apparent to others.

After my year on the Montrose APA 212, we made our way back to New London where I had been accepted for my Sub School training, and since Pat was pregnant, we were assigned to the limited officers' quarters on the base. This was conveniently located across the street from the golf course, and I had the only pregnant caddie in town.

When Pat's big day came, she was in labor for many hours, and as I was holding her hand, voicing my encouragement, she was out of it. She kept calling me nurse, and I had to keep telling her that I wasn't her nurse, I was her husband. After twenty hours in labor—must have been a world record—our beautiful little girl Pamela was born. We were the happiest parents in the world at that moment.

From sub school, our next few years were spent with my being at sea off and on again on the Redfin SSR 272, and a new son, Tom, was born in Norfolk while I was at sea. Pat was a great Navy wife, who could handle the home front while I was gone, and then some. After being at sea for a few weeks, we came home on a Saturday and expected to go back out on Monday. However, we soon learned that Vice-Admiral Grenfell, ComSubLant (commander of submarines in the Atlantic), and his wife were hosting an open house at the officer's club on Sunday afternoon and that attendance was mandatory. Ugh!

We weren't happy with this interruption of our home time, but we dressed up and obediently went. After parking the car and going up the steps to the club, I opened the door for Pat to go in. Immediately, I heard, "Hi Pat," and as I walked in, there was the Admiral and Mrs. Grenfell, greeting everyone as they came in the door. I was in shock, as you could imagine. How did the Admiral know my wife? After talking pleasantries there, we walked in as I was dying to find out how the Admiral knew my wife.

It turns out, while I was gone, Pat had organized a committee of officers' wives to help enlisted wives with problems while their husbands were at sea, a favorite program of the admiral's. That was Pat, helping others and making an impact with all who met her, even an admiral. He later presented her with a letter of appreciation.

When I left the Navy after my five years of obligated service, we moved to Baltimore where I started my career in manufacturing with Procter and Gamble. During our years there, Pat delivered a second daughter, Linda, to round out our family.

In Baltimore, the night before Halloween was "mischief night." I was watching a ball game on TV and oblivious to this mischief stuff, but our oldest daughter, Pam, saw a group of boys with flashlights coming down the alley behind the house. They were turning over all the trash cans. Pam ran down the stairs to tell her mom in the kitchen about the trash can event happening behind our house. Pat immediately went out the back door and turned on the garden hose. The next thing that I know, she's walking into the family room, the egg is in her hair and running down her face. "Pat, what happened to you?"

Pat said, "They didn't get my trash can."

"What do you mean, they didn't get your trash can?" The explanation, had me shaking my head. Pat's competitive spirit was amazing, taking on twenty boys and driving them away with a water hose—she wet them down well, but got egged in the process!

After five delightful years in Baltimore, and then two in Cincinnati, we were transferred to Long Beach, California. My good friend and neighbor Ralph Adams called to tell me what he saw out his front window. "You won't believe what I saw. Pat was walking down the sidewalk when the boys who were shooting baskets on a backboard attached to the garage saw her. One of them flipped the ball out to Pat and said, 'Take a shot, Mrs. Paulk.' She did too, nothing but net! Then she kept on walking down the sidewalk while the boys were in shock that this woman could nonchalantly make a shot like that." Unbeknownst to them, Pat had played basketball in high school and, apparently, had not lost her touch.

Pat loved to entertain and did so often. She also got involved in her church by serving as the finance director and superintendent of Sunday schools. She was elected president of the local PTA and organized events for them. She also served as president of a homeowners board for ten years.

When our children were out of school, she decided to sell real estate and was very successful with a loyal following. It wasn't long before she was on the local board of realtors, and then she was elected president of the Huntington Beach/Fountain Valley board with a membership of 2,500 realtors. She was on the California State Board and national board. Had she been inclined, she could have gone into politics, but she had no desire to do that.

Over the years we had some great vacations, but the best, by far, was a long trip to Lizard Island in Australia, which sits almost on the Great Barrier Reef. Pat was in paradise. She snorkeled off the beaches to reach the nearby reefs and totally immersed herself in the myriad schools of multicolored fish.

We fished on a charter boat while there and caught sailfish, dorado, barracuda, and giant trevally. When we returned to the anchorage area, the captain told us to watch as he banged on the side of the boat and held this twenty-pound barracuda over the side. Suddenly a huge fish came up and swallowed that fish like it was a minnow! We later learned that the big fish was a potato cod, a member of the grouper family that likely weighed more than three hundred pounds. The resort there prepared our dorado (mahi-mahi) for the guests that evening, a special way to finish off a day of fishing just off the Great Barrier Reef.

For over twenty-five years in California, we had an offshore sportfishing boat, *Kingfisher*, and a partnership with a neighbor, Glenn Tisman, in the ownership of mooring #126 in Avalon Harbor on Catalina Island, located twenty-six miles off the coast of southern California. Pat loved to fish, maybe not as much as me, but she learned to catch striped marlin and other fish, large and small. Having caught a marlin, she proudly and often wore a silver marlin on her neck chain. Since we had guests aboard frequently, she learned to operate the boat while I helped our guests fish.

Pat's greatest fishing accomplishment was catching a 110-pound bigeye tuna on a thirty-pound monofilament line. She fought that fish for one and a half hours before I could get a gaff in it. When she would pump the fish up, it would see the boat, spook, and go for the bottom. This happened repeatedly. Finally, we got it aboard and took it to the green pier in Avalon, where Rosie, our weighmaster, could get the official weight. Yes, indeed, Pat had caught the largest tuna by a woman angler in southern California—quite an achievement. She also caught the largest albacore tuna for the year, and it had been a good year for men and women. She truly earned many awards, and after the bigeye, she could barely lift her arms for days. It was like lifting weights.

I believe our love continued to grow throughout our marriage because of the trust, admiration, and respect we had for one another. We were never competitive, unless we were playing ping pong. In fact, we helped and supported each other with all the strength we had. She was an angel with an unbelievable aura I found on the campus of the University of Delaware, when we were so young, and it never went away. It was always there, and the love for her has never waned, even though she has been gone for five years now. I told her to vote me into Heaven, because there is no doubt that's where she is. I have always felt that she was beautiful, inside and out, and I was so fortunate to be married to her for almost sixty years. Yep, this old Georgia boy married way over his head. She was a winner in life, if there ever was one. I love her so much!

A couple at USNA—Pat and Jim at USNA during their junior year after their engagement.

Wedding dress—Pat at the wedding reception at the Old Mill.

Swords—Sword
ceremony; left, top-
down: Mike Reu,
Tom Marnane, Ron
Marryott; center: Pat
and Jim; right, top-
down: Warren
Zimmer, Earl Piper,
and Carl Croft.

Big ring—Pat and
Jim at the Ring
ceremony.

Pat and Jim are welcomed aboard the cruise ship, *Constitution.*

Bobby Paulk (younger brother), Wes in the boat with binoculars, and Jim with a blue marlin caught during a cruise stop in Kona.

CRUISING

C RUISING, AS IN GOING ON A CRUISE. There is more to it than just going on a cruise to drink and to see how fat you can get from all the food without much exercise! This story was written initially as a letter to the family of Betty and Wes Bannister, two great friends on their fiftieth wedding anniversary. We missed them so much since moving to my roots in southeast Georgia and regretted that we could not be a part of the festivities as they celebrated their anniversary.

Oh, the stories we could tell—but won't! We tried to go down memory lane with a few pictures and stories of some great vacations we had together for them to share. When you stop and think about it, how many couples want to share a whole week with another couple (friends) in a distant place, away from the comforts of home? Not many! We will always cherish our relationship with them and happily remember our fun times together. We also sent pictures of some of our trips together for the family album that would be given to the couple at the celebration.

These adventures included a cruise around the Hawaiian

Islands onboard the USS Constitution (1), a week's vacation in Port Washington (2), a week in southeast Georgia (3), and adventures in a Bluebird Motor home (see Orville), just to name a few. (For the record, these and others became separate stories for our book).

My brother, Bobby, and wife, Vila, friends Buddy and Dot Bright, Guy and Shirley Cheek (all from Georgia), and Jack Robertson joined us on the USS Constitution for a cruise around the Hawaiian Islands. We had a wonderful time together and had so many laughs. During our first evening meal, our group was placed at two tables, but when we asked our waiter to put the tables together, he did so promptly.

Then, after we were seated and during introductions, since many in our group didn't know one another, the waiter overheard me saying, "Wes is the mayor of Huntington Beach, and we are going to have him run for Governor of California." Later, the maître d' returned after Wes and Betty had left the table and discretely asked for their names and cabin number. Our cabin was right next door to theirs, and when we returned to ours, we knocked on their door and told them we had given their cabin number to the maître d' at his request. He was probably thinking either Wes was governor of California or next in line to be so.

They thanked us very kindly, haha! Sure enough, the next morning, they had a special invitation under their door inviting them to the captain's stateroom that evening for a private cocktail party and dinner in his cabin. They got even with us though. When they heard at dinner the captain of the ship was a graduate of the Chinese Naval Academy, they informed him that not only had I attended the Naval Academy, but that I retired as an Admiral! (Not true.)

Then, not only did we get an invitation for cocktails and dinner the next evening in his cabin, but I was asked to report to the bridge every time the ship made port or got underway so I could tell him what a good job he did maneuvering the ship—often before 7:00 a.m. I think the captain enjoyed all of us so much, we were included in all his cocktail parties. Thereafter, I had to get up at 5:00 a.m. a few times as we entered port, on vacation!

After arranging the cruise, we reserved a car and a van at each port so we could split up to do different things. Another reservation was for a boat in Kona to fish blue marlin which turned out to be a successful one. I fought one for over two hours on a light line, with Wes holding a knife threatening to cut the line so he could get a fish too. When the captain heard we had caught a 317-pound fish, he wanted to know why we hadn't brought it back to the ship. "We could have fed everyone on the entire ship with it."

One thing we learned about Wes during that trip was that he truly enjoys adventures and doing the unexpected, especially when traveling. He'd say, "Let's see what's down this road," even though there were signs advising us not to travel that way! For example, as he drove around the big island, taking some of those roads that were ill-advised with clearly printed signs, we saw some beautiful scenery. At one stop, he walked out on an older lava flow, potentially over lava tubes, far beyond the forbidden signs. He wanted to see where the lava dropped off into the ocean and the rest of us went along too, despite the danger signs. We walked about a mile from the road where the old lava flowed over and the steam rising from the lava as it fell into the ocean was spectacular, though a bit dangerous. We did see some sights that we wouldn't have seen if it hadn't been for Wes, but maybe we shouldn't let him drive so much.

Posing with
fish—Jerry
Coleman, Pat with
champagne, Jim.

Rosie Cadman
weighing the
big marlin.

Hoisted fish—Fish being hoisted on
the green pier from *Kingfisher*.

MY OLD MAN AND THE SEA STORY

W E HAD FAVORITE SPOTS TO FISH, but one key to know before you left the dock was where marlin and lots of bait had been seen. With the latest intelligence in hand, Pat and I headed south out of Huntington Beach, California, with a young man from Atlanta, Jerry Coleman, who had never caught a marlin before, and my goal for the day was to put him on one.

Nothing happened until late in the afternoon, when we hooked a big fish on a jig behind the boat for Jerry, but he came off. I said, "I'm going back around, Pat, it's your turn." Well, he bit again, but shortly, came unbuttoned too. So, I said, "I'm going around again to see if I can get him to go again. My turn." Sure enough, he bit and I pushed the throttles forward as I always did to set the hook with the boat.

Then I throttled back and went down from the flying bridge into the cockpit, and let Pat take the controls while I took the rod out of the rod holder. When that fish jumped, we could see that he was a monster, and with thirty-pound test line, we had a fight on our hands. I started reeling as fast as I could.

When we had a fish on, I liked to fight it from the bow pulpit with toes under the toe rail to hold on with my feet so that both arms were free to "yank and crank!" The captain could also maneuver the boat better going forward than backing down. So, I carefully made my way to the bow along the side of the boat, holding the rod in one hand and the grab rail with the other, and began what I knew would be a long process. Pat did a great job of running the boat so I wouldn't get spooled and, gradually, I started to gain line that the fish had ripped off the reel.

At first, we had to regain about three hundred yards of line that went off the reel after the fish was hooked in the initial run. We started with 550 yards when we began the fight. So, Pat moved the boat slowly in the direction the fish was jumping, and I reeled as fast as I could to keep the line tight and regain line. We were constantly changing boat direction to follow this powerful fish. As fast as I got the line back on the reel, he would rip it off again. If I allowed any slack in the line, I knew that we might lose him.

At one point, he started a run at the boat which was a decisive moment in the fight. However, I started reeling as fast as I could while I asked Pat to turn the boat away from the fish to help me keep the line tight. Close call, but we soon regained control and avoided losing him. From that point on, he would rip line off the reel, change direction, and I was doing all I could to crank on the fish and give Pat instructions so we could work together. Watching a fish this large make a series of jumps, was a beautiful sight. Sometimes it was a single jump completely out of the water. We were thrilled to watch the show the fish was giving us. It seemed to me as if this fish had been hooked before and knew how to get away. He was sure testing my ability as an angler.

After an hour and a half, we finally had the fish at the boat, and the first task was to get the fish motor out of the water (the tail). With a gaff, we stuck it near the tail, lifted it up, and put a tail rope on it. Then the three of us tried to pull it into the boat, but try as we might, we couldn't do it. It wasn't the weight of the fish, but the length that gave us the problem.

We tried time after time without success and finally decided we would have to tow it to Catalina to be weighed in. I knew it would take time to tow it slowly to the island, but when I tried calling the Harbor Master to ask Rosie, the weigh master on the Green pier in Avalon Bay, to wait for us, the mountain on the east end of Catalina blocked me out, and I couldn't get through.

However, a friend, legendary marlin fisherman, and fishing club member, Ed Martin, was directly outside of the island on the Avalon Bank and heard me on the radio. When he came up, I asked him if he could relay my message to Rosie for me because we were going to be late getting in with that fish. Thankfully, he did that for us, and it relieved the pressure on us in getting the fish in before Rosie shut down for the day. But after a few more minutes, I started thinking about Ernest Hemingway and his story, *The Old Man and the Sea*. You may recall that the poor old man lost his fish to the sharks after getting the big fish (blue marlin) tied to the side of his small boat.

I sure didn't want that to be the end of our story too. So, I stopped the boat and said that I wanted to add a second tail rope, which we did. Now, Jerry had a Black Belt and was a very strong young man, but the three of us couldn't get the fish aboard with one rope. With two ropes tied around the fish's tail, Jerry pulled on one while Pat and I pulled on the other one, and we got it in the boat. The head and bill went up one side while the tail was up at the other side of the *Kingfisher*'s cockpit. I taped the mouth closed with duct tape so that it wouldn't hang open when we weighed it in. Then we hauled tail for the Green Pier in Avalon.

I knew that there would be a crowd awaiting us because the custom was to fire a small cannon on the pier to alert people in town that a fish was coming to be weighed with the information to be recorded on the weight board there. The rumor was out that it was a huge fish, and I was just hoping that I didn't wreck the boat in front of the large crowd as I was anxiously backing the boat in and getting it tied up. Rosie always roped off the weigh area to give us plenty of room to weigh the fish and take photos without interference from all the people.

Rosie lowered the hoist rope down, and we connected the tail so that she could hoist it and put it on the scale. It was 219.5 pounds, a huge fish for SoCal, and we had heard of only one larger which might have been a blue marlin instead of a striped one. We were given the normal bottle of champagne and photos with a board listing angler, captain, and gaffer on it for the photo op. For comparison purposes, a large marlin in local waters was 175–180 pounds, while most were 125–150 pounds.

That was not quite the end of the story. When Pat and I arrived at the trophy dinner in January at a Huntington Beach country club, the trophy chairman came over as we entered the room and whispered, "I hope you have plenty of room in your trunk." Well, the perpetual trophies were about three feet tall, and a nice plaque came with each award which the angler could keep. When the ceremony started—and we started winning awards—I was so embarrassed, I wanted to climb under the table. I won't list each award we received but catching this big fish on the light line was a recognized accomplishment. Let's leave it at that.

After dinner, several friends helped us get the trophies in the car. On one hand, we were delighted with the awards, but on the other, we felt selfish too. Strange, but real.

No doubt about it, catching this big fish was one of the highlights of our angling years on the *Kingfisher*, and certainly, one that I'll never forget because so many were involved in this entire event. Rosie Cadman had a fish and chips shack on the pier and with her outgoing personality, she was a key fixture of Catalina Island and friend to everyone.

As a postscript to the story: Yes, we got Jerry a fish on a subsequent trip.

Tuna fishing rod on
left—Bob McNary,
Jim, and Irv Friedman.

Pat's Tuna—Jim and
Pat with *Kingfisher*
in the background.

Tuna fishing rod on right—Bob McNary,
Jim, and Irv Friedman.

THE BIGEYE TUNA CHALLENGE

T HIS IS A BIG, BIG TUNA STORY. If you spend enough time
on the water, you see and do things that are seemingly
impossible, but when it's over, it leaves an impression that never
goes away. You remember it forever. This is that kind of a story.

Our neighbor Gunter was a sail boater, not a fisherman, but he
had brought his sailboat to our mooring 126 in Avalon Bay on
Catalina Island, twenty-six miles off the coast of Southern
California. While our two boats were side tied one evening, we
told him that the three of us on *Kingfisher* were going fishing early
the next morning, but that we would return by 6:00 p.m., and join
them on their boat for hors d'oeuvres and a glass of wine. That
was the grand plan.

With anticipation for a fun day on the water, and maybe get a
chance to pull on striped marlin, we pulled out of the harbor early
as planned and headed around the east end of the island. We were
headed for an ocean "high spot" where the bottom peaked out a
few hundred feet below the surface, about ten miles off the back-
side of the island.

With the twin diesel engines cranked up, we cruised the *Kingfisher* at twenty-eight knots with my two anglers Bob, a retired pilot with Continental Airlines, and Irv, a teacher at Westminster High School, ready to do battle with a big one. I had an experienced fishing crew.

We were all on the flybridge with binoculars in hand looking for any signs of bird or sea life. With twenty-five or thirty pieces of live bait (nice-sized green mackerel) swimming in the live bait tank, we hoped to toss one in front of a tailing fish (a fish on the top of the water with only the tail exposed, we called them tailers) or to a fish rising to the lures we were trolling. The consensus of fishermen was that a bait-hooked fish was less likely to come "unbuttoned" than a jig-hooked one. So, we had a live bait rigged on a swivel in the cockpit bait tank ready to go. We also had a similarly rigged bait in the bow bait tank and it too, was ready to throw.

We were rigged and ready when we arrived at the high spot and noted there were no other boats around. So, it appeared we had managed to sneak out of the harbor without any other boats following us. We also planned to stay off the radio to prevent other boats from getting a radio directional fix on us.

We began the monotonous trolling drill, with two of us on the bridge, and one in the cockpit watching the jigs as they rode the tops of waves. They were placed specifically to not tangle when we turned the boat and were always a beautiful sight as they darted about, up and down, pushing water with their dished-out front end to attract fish. Our lure colors were based upon weather conditions, cloudy or clear skies. I was partial to a black and purple one, and usually had one in the mix.

As the day became another day of looking for birds working over a fish or reeling in a jig to remove a piece of kelp that prevented it from working properly, the routine was established. Everyone had a job to do and had to be ready as this kind of fishing went from pure boredom to chaos instantly. Throwing a bait, dropping one back into the lure pattern, or clearing the other fishing rigs out of the water so they wouldn't get tangled with the line with a fish on it—it was lots to do, quickly and calmly, so mistakes were not made. When a fish hit a jig, as we called a lure, I would push the throttles forward to set the hook and keep the line tight using the boat while the anglers were clearing the other rods out of the way.

As the day went on, with no action, we moved around to various high spots, looking for sea life, any kind, but it appeared we were in a desert. We had to chalk it up as another day of "experience," like so many other unsuccessful fishing days. At times, you could fish for days and not even see a fish, much less get one to pull on.

So, I told the guys, "We're going to make a short run to fish near the backside of the island, near Catalina Harbor, for a few last tries. Reel the lines in." When we got to the spot where I wanted to work, we slowed the boat down and put the lines back out. I made a few passes over the area I wanted to check out and noted that our time was about up We'd need to haul tail to get back on the mooring by six, as promised to Gunter. "Okay guys, last pass and then we'll need to 'crank 'em in' to get back on time."

As I looked back at the darting jigs we had placed on various waves, I saw a large fish suddenly, and violently, hit the jig on the third wave back, and I instantly pushed the throttles forward to set the hook firmly. Right after, I saw another fish take the jig on the second wave—close to the boat, and just as violently. It appeared to be a large brown fish, certainly not a marlin.

As a boat moves forward, it creates rolling waves behind it, maybe fifteen to twenty feet or so apart, and lures work best on the front, top of the waves. Placement of the lures behind a moving boat to be most effective must be placed on the top front section of the waves created by the motion of the boat and so that they don't tangle when the boat turns. We had five lines out when the first fish hit.

When that first fish hit, pulling the line out of the outrigger, it was like a race car wreck—instant excitement, very loud, as it popped loose from the outrigger, adrenaline pumping, line screaming off the reel, and hearts beating extra fast! When that second fish hit, we had two fish on and three other lines to get in. The line I had running back from the bridge, was down the middle of the set, the farthest back. I got it in when the two fish were firmly hooked, and got the boat slowed down. Then I went down the ladder, into the cockpit where my two anglers were holding on for dear life as the line was ripping off their reels, fast—making a zinging sound which created fear that the fish would take all the line and say goodbye. We called this "getting spooled"!

When I got the other two lines in, and the rods out of the way, I knew we were in for a long, tough fight. Since neither fish jumped, I knew we hadn't hooked up a couple of marlin, but I didn't know what we had on. I just hoped it wasn't a couple of mako sharks that come to these waters to give birth, away from males which would eat the babies.

My wife and I hooked a huge mako once that likely weighed several hundred pounds on a marlin jig. After a forty-five-minute battle with the fish, we got her to the boat, but Pat couldn't get a flying gaff in her tough skin. After another fifteen minutes, we got a second shot at gaffing her, like "hold my beer, and I'll show you how to do it." Smartass—I couldn't get the gaff in her either! And with her thrashing and twisting, she finally bit through the leader line, and was gone. After thinking about it, we decided that losing her was probably the best outcome too. We really didn't need that big fish with all those teeth thrashing around in the boat.

So, were we in for another shark fight? We didn't know. I had set the drags (pressure to pull line off the reel) with a drag scale for accuracy on the thirty-pound line we had on the reels, at seven and a half pounds, but by pushing the drag levers all the way forward, you would have fifteen pounds of drag.

I went back up to the bridge to turn the boat to get after the fish so the anglers could recover some line. After about fifteen to twenty minutes, things had settled down a little, and we were breathing normally again. The good thing was we had recovered enough line so we were in no danger of getting spooled now.

However, after about thirty more minutes of "yanking and cranking," we still weren't exactly sure what we were fighting. I had one angler on the bow saying, "Go! He's ripping line off again." The angler in the cockpit, with his fish going in the opposite direction, said the same thing, "Go!" Obviously, this was a dilemma, if I went in either direction, we would lose one of the fish. So, I told both to push the drag levers all the way forward to slow them down with the additional pressure on the fish—which it did, and we worked to get both anglers back in the cockpit. We had to do a little "over and under rod drill" to keep the lines from getting together. After an hour of fighting these fish, we got the first fish to the boat, got two gaffs in it, and pulled it into the boat. It was rare, for these waters—a bigeye tuna! It was the first one ever caught on our boat, the *Kingfisher*.

In the meantime, the fight went on with the second fish, and after a couple of hours of pumping the fish up from the depths, it continued to see the boat and head for the bottom again. Then, to add to this drama, a huge shark started circling around, he clearly was looking for a free meal.

After two hours and forty minutes, we finally got the second fish to the side of the boat, got two gaffs in it, and pulled it into the boat—before the shark got him. That was a mighty big relief because of the challenges we faced. I had my doubts at times that we would get them, but we did. As always, fighting and landing two fish, hooked simultaneously, took good teamwork, and we needed it.

In the meantime, Gunter was very anxious that we hadn't returned yet, and he got off the mooring to go look for us. He started out west in his sailboat (wrong direction, as it turned out). Not finding us, he returned to the harbor and contacted the Harbor Patrol, "Jim said he would be back at six, but he's not here, and we are very concerned because Jim always does what he says."

The Harbor Patrol responded, "Don't worry about Jim, he's at the pier now weighing in the two biggest tuna that you have ever seen." So, what did they weigh? One was one hundred pounds and the other was and 121 pounds, nice fish, and a couple of exhausted and satisfied anglers had big smiles on their faces as we returned to the mooring for "cocktail hour." This had been a very happy day, indeed.

To put a punctuation mark on this story, Pat and I, with just the two of us on the boat, hooked up at my secret spot the next weekend. She caught a 110-pound bigeye that took her an hour and a half to get. Catching a bigeye tuna is like lifting weights when the fish would spook at the boat and head for the bottom, time after time. Pat desperately tried to give me the rod, but it was her fish to fight, and I wasn't about to take that accomplishment away from her.

Jed Welsh, the legendary writer for the *Long Beach Press-Telegram*, called them gorillas, and we weren't about to argue with him. These fish were tough fighters. Though she couldn't lift her arms for a couple of days—true story—Pat got her fish and the award for first and largest tuna of the year for a woman angler in Southern California. The captain? Well, he always enjoyed watching and helping others get the fish of a lifetime with a big smile on his face. And that was the way it was!

SURVIVING A STORM

B OB MCNARY AND I heard that marlin were being caught at Santa Barbara Island, and with this reliable information, we decided to make the, approximately, fifty-mile run overnight out to the island and get the jigs in the water at daylight the next morning. *Kingfisher*, our boat named after the bird, was in good shape, and we had a week's worth of provisions onboard and a full load of diesel. The only thing missing was a full bait tank. Stopping at an oil island inside the Los Angeles Harbor at about 10:00 p.m., we started jigging with our rigs of four hooks hidden in feathers, they were called "Lucky Joe" rigs. In no time at all, we had twenty-five to thirty pieces of bait (live mackerel, about a pound each) swimming around in the bait tank. Now ready to head northwest, I told Bob to go below to get some rest, I'll make the run from the flybridge.

About all I can remember about this trip was how peaceful it was anchored in the lee of the island after a hard day looking for fish, and the ease of replacing mackerel that had been used or died in the bait tank. I can't remember if we caught fish on this trip, but we did catch and release marlin there on many trips to the island. That is not relevant to this story, but the decision to go back to Avalon to refuel was relevant. Stay tuned!

As Bob and I were making the twenty-five-mile run to Catalina Island and onto our mooring #126 in Avalon Harbor, we were discussing how nice and calm the ocean had been. Then, as we rounded the east end of Catalina, our "delightful" weather suddenly changed, and we were hit in the face by a strong, gale-force wind. Not good.

I said to Bob, "Better get those rods out of the rocket launcher rod holder on the back of the flybridge down to the salon area and come back up." In the meantime, I'm holding the flybridge bimini cover with one hand and the boat's helm (wheel) with the other. The loss of the Bimini was a real concern, and I was afraid that if it went, it could cause a lot of damage as it blew away, maybe even take me with it. Then, another incident scared the daylights out of me. Something heavy hit me in the small of the back, hard, very hard, and at the same time, I got this strong fishy smell. At that instant, the two things didn't make sense to me. Still holding onto the Bimini top and the wheel, I looked behind me and saw a huge flying fish on the deck that the strong wind had launched higher and faster than normal to hit me up on the flybridge! I couldn't let go of anything to grab the fish but managed to kick it off the boat, a lucky maneuver.

When Bob came back up after stowing the nine rods below, we had to make some decisions—critical ones. In the middle of a very bad storm with wind out of the southwest and seas over five feet with whitecaps, we had no immediate shelter except our mooring which was in the lee of the casino, so that was where we were headed, we had to get out of this wind and reach safety. On the way, we passed the "Can Dump," the burning trash from Avalon residents there always smelled the same. Bad. Avalon and safety were just ahead.

However, that was not to be. The harbor patrol informed us that the harbor was closed, no one could enter or leave until the storm was over. Oh no, now what? We had very little fuel and the way we were getting bounced around, any particulate matter at the bottom of the tanks could get stirred up in the fuel tanks and clog the fuel filters enough to shut the engines down, or we could simply run out of fuel, marking the end of *Kingfisher* and maybe us too. We put on life jackets as I told Bob, "Now is the time to calmly think about the actions we need to take to survive this dangerous storm." I did the best I could to find the safest course direction as we did at sea in the Navy, then tried not to fall—it was rough!

Our view of the harbor from outside was chaos, boats were being pushed together, a sailboat was dragging its anchor across the harbor entrance with no one aboard. The harbor patrol was dragging it back, but the anchor would not grab. So, they had to constantly drag it around to keep it from damaging other boats. The big double-deck boat, that ferried people back and forth to the island, was not allowed to enter the harbor either. It was motoring around in front of the harbor entrance.

We talked about running back to Catalina Harbor on the back-side of the island, but I didn't know if I had enough fuel to get there, and then come back to Avalon – no fuel at Cat Harbor as we called it. We certainly weren't going to head for home with our fuel condition. After discussing options, I decided to get away from the entrance and the chaos occurring there.

We went outside a few miles and picked courses that rattled us and the boat the least while staying in contact with the Harbor Patrol. During my radio contact with them, another voice popped up on the radio, Bob Norman, who worked as a crewman on swordfish boats. He told me that he was there for me, and for the next couple of hours, he gave us a report on harbor conditions. He had been in very bad shape and having had numerous cancer surgeries, he had his mattress on the floor of the living room of his apartment, where he could watch TV and have a clear view of the harbor. Talking with Bob while we were bouncing around, holding the Bimini down, was extremely comforting. Somebody cared about two wayward sailors fighting to survive in this rare windstorm, and though there wasn't much he could do for us, he was there to help in any way he could. Very good to know!

Eventually, the wind seemed to abate some, to maybe forty miles an hour, and I started trying to get the harbor patrol to let us sneak in behind the short breakwater and the casino which shielded our mooring there. Soon, they came back on the radio, "There's another boat on your mooring."

I said, "What's the name on the boat."

Harbor patrol called back, "Blue Lagoon, or something like that."

"Never heard of it."

"They had the permission of the owner."

I said, "I'm the owner and we have been fishing up at Santa Barbara for three days and I didn't give permission to anyone to use the mooring."

Harbor patrol replied, "Your wife said that you were fishing up at Santa Barbara and didn't need it."

"We'll have to side-tie with them, and may need your help."

"*Kingfisher*, please do what I tell you," as we listened to the harbor master upon entering Avalon Bay to avoid the danger there.

These conditions posed a real challenge because we didn't know what obstacles would be in our way. As we started in, I asked Bob to get six fenders we had stowed under the helm area down to the cockpit, and when we get in a bit of a lee, start tying them off on the starboard side and get the lines ready to tie-off on the other boat.

Now we expected the owners of this mystery boat to be onboard to help us, but as I went past them and twisted the boat around in a very small area, it was very clear—no one was aboard. Things were going against us this trip for sure. To make matters worse, that boat was not a fishing boat like ours. It was a tri-cabin job with very high sides, which made it hard to reach when trying to get our lines aboard her.

To secure our boat to theirs we needed a line to their bow from ours, one to their stern from ours, and two lines rigged fore and aft to hold the boats in place. There was wind to deal with, but we managed to get the lines secure and six large fenders hanging between the boats. Now what? We were mentally and physically exhausted, had nothing to eat for a long time, and we needed rest more than food at that point, to tell the truth.

I can't remember what time it was, but it was late as the owner of the boat and his group finally returned from a night of partying in Avalon. They offered us the left-over food from dinner which we gladly accepted, and as it turned out, the owner was a member of our church, a nice guy. The story? While they were having a good time, we were fighting for our lives. We survived though, took on fuel the next morning, and headed for home.

Maybe we needed a bigger boat!

CATCHING AN AIRPLANE

T HIS IS A TRUE STORY, and whether you believe it or not, airplanes can be very catchable at times. Often over the years, when not fishing, we were on our mooring (a floating ball with lines attached for tying up a boat fore and aft) #126, it was anchored with a large concrete block near the fuel dock in Avalon Harbor on Catalina Island. On a beautiful day, not a cloud in the sky, we were relaxing in the cockpit of our boat, *Kingfisher*, named after a bird that I loved to watch as a youngster. The boat that we owned for over twenty-five years was a thirty-four-foot Tollycraft, equipped with twin, 225 horsepower, diesel engines, and all the electronics needed for an offshore sportfishing boat.

Our friend, Gene Duchene, came by for a visit in his small Avon inflatable he kept on his boat, *MY MARIE*—named for his wife, Marie. Over the years, Gene and I fished and socialized together many times. With both of us so passionate about fishing, our kids had decided at one point, that we should know one another. Their "conspiracy" worked. We became very close friends for life and good fishing buddies.

Gene, looking up at me from his dinghy, said, "Would you like to go around the east end to see if we can catch some seabass?"

My reply was, "Absolutely!"

Gene said, "I'll get my gear and come back to pick you up."

East end referred to a short move around the east end of Catalina Island, and seabass were white seabass, a great eating fish. Prize catches by anglers.

So, I got my fishing gear ready. Shortly, Gene came back for me, and we were soon out of the harbor, which was full of boats, on their moorings. We decided we might as well troll our way along the Catalina shoreline to see what might jump on our lines on our leisurely ride. It was a beautiful day, no surprise in southern California—we had lots of them. No wind either and, hopefully, it would stay calm so we wouldn't get wet in that little boat.

Gene tied on a yellow/gold Scampi, and I tied on a mackerel-colored CD eighteen Rapala jig. We were fishing and talking. Gene had his line out on the starboard side, facing the island, and I was trolling on the port side facing the ocean—an important element for this story. As I was watching for any bird activity that might indicate larger fish pushing baitfish to the surface and look-ing over Gene's left shoulder, I saw what appeared to be a lone bird several miles out from us. No feeding activity, only flying in our direction.

We weren't having any luck, but naturally, I kept watching that bird since it was the only thing that was in my view. Then it started getting bigger as it neared us, and I could see it was an ultralight airplane. I remarked to Gene, "This is crazy, why would an ultralight be out here?" As it got closer and closer, we could see that it was equipped with pontoons. It seemed to be flying lower and lower. "Gene, that thing looks like it's going to land on the water!" Then, surprisingly, it was on the water. We couldn't believe this!

Gene said, "We better go out there to see what's going on," and I agreed. After reeling in our lines, we headed out. He was maybe a mile and a half out from us.

When we got to him, I said, "How are you doing?"

He replied, "Okay."

"What are you doing out here?" Gene said.

"I'm working with a swordfish boat," he said. "Flying around, looking for swordfish on the surface. I was just talking with them on my two-way radio, and they are about an hour and a half away and coming to pick me up. I ran out of gas."

We were accustomed to swordfish boats we called "stick boats." They often worked with a spotter plane who shared in the profits of the swordfish boat—but ultralights? This was a first for us. An airplane was a handy and common tool for finding fish instead of relying on spotting them from the lower height of the boat tower. They could cover a wide area of water faster than the boat, and after radioing the location of the fish, they would circle the fish to guide the boat to the fish.

During the process, as the plane directed the boat to the fish, the boat would carefully approach from the front of the fish. If the boat came at the fish from the back or side, the fish would spook and go down. However, the bow-on direction worked because swordfish are fearless. They aren't afraid of anything they might encounter in the ocean. The crewman with a harpoon would go out on the long-bow plank of the boat, and when over the fish, he would hit him with the harpoon. The tip of the harpoon would then release from the shaft, and with it tied to a ball float, the boat would leave to look for other swordfish. Later, they would come back to retrieve the fish after it was safer to do so (swordfish were dangerous when alive).

Back to the ultralight, Gene said to the young man sitting in the open ultralight, "It might be kind of dangerous sitting out here with no power, and the wind coming up. Would you like us to tow you into Avalon where you could safely tie up to a mooring?"

He said, "That would be great, I'd really appreciate it." Funny, we never exchanged names—maybe because it could have been a perilous situation, and we were in a hurry to get him to safety.

Gene asked, "Do you have a rope?" But he didn't have one.

The inflatable had a short rope tied to the bow and was the only way we could secure the boat and plane together. After tying the dinghy to a pontoon cleat on the ultralight, we set out for Avalon, we looked like a couple of crabs going through the water sideways, but it worked. Thankfully, we didn't have far to go.

When we got to Avalon, the harbor patrol boat on duty outside the harbor, came over quickly to see what was going on with this weird-looking tow operation. We explained the situation to him, and with a decent tow line, he tied the ultralight to an outside buoy to await the arrival of his stick boat, which would lift the ultralight on its deck and head for home: San Diego. Since it was tied to an outside mooring buoy, the boat would have no problem accessing it.

For us, we decided to have a little fun and go to the Green Pier to make our report to Rosie, who was the official weighmaster. She weighed marlin when boats brought them in. The information: boat name, captain, weight, and date were ceremonially listed on the marlin board on the side of the fish and chips shack where everyone walking the pier could see which boat had the most fish or the largest one. There was an annual contest where the boat who caught the largest marlin of the year would receive an award for their achievement. We didn't know if there was an airplane category, but it would be fun with Rosie for sure.

When we got to the pier and had her attention, Gene said, "Rosie, we are here to report the catch of the first and largest airplane of the year. There it is." We pointed to the plane tied off at the mooring where the harbor patrol had put it. We were grinning ear to ear.

Rosie, with a big smile on her face and shaking her head, said, "You guys are always full of it."

We were indeed, but this was definitely an unexpected fun outcome of a fishing trip. Later, we saw the swordfish boat pick up the poor airplane rescued by a couple of wise guys in a small inflatable. No fish, but it was a fun adventure for Gene and me.

Marlin—Jim,
Gene Duchane,
and Bob McNary.

Wahoo—Gene
Duchane with a
wahoo in Jim's
backyard.

DELIVERING A SAILBOAT

O N A FRIDAY AFTERNOON, my neighbor from across the street came into my garage where I was busy working on a typical home project. Gunter Lieder, originally from Germany, had emigrated to this country, learned to speak English after he got here, and prospered.

"Guess what?" Gunter said.

I repied with a smile on my face, of course, "With you, I have no clue."

"I bought a new sailboat!"

"What did you get?" Since I was a power boater, I didn't know a lot about sailboats.

Gunter replied, "It's a thirty-two-foot Islander, sloop-rigged, and I need some help bringing it to Huntington Beach, California, from the Long Beach Marina. Can you give me a hand?"

"When do you plan to get it?" I asked.

Gunter said, "In the morning, and I was wondering if Pat might drive us over there?"

"Sure, I'll check with Pat to see if she is available. That would be fun and wouldn't take all day either." Mistake number one.

When my wife, Pat, agreed to drive us to the Long Beach Marina at 9:00 a.m. the next morning, we were all set to begin our first sailing adventure together, although I expected we would motor the short distance to Gunter's slip so he could get it prepared for sailing.

As it turned out, both of our wives dropped us off at about nine Saturday morning at the Long Beach Marina where the sales office and boat were located. Our plan was to complete the paperwork, get checked out on the boat, then cruise the short distance back to Huntington Beach to put the boat into a slip near mine. After completing the paperwork, it was placed in a large, page-sized, brown envelope, an important point (don't forget this), and we walked down to a nearby slip to have an inspection and indoctrination of the new boat. This would be my first look at Gunter's new boat.

During the checkout of the boat, the dealer showed us how to start the small diesel engine. The engine started up but shut off after a couple of minutes which was a little alarming. Mistake number two.

What's with this problem? I thought. The dealer said that sometimes the fuel line gets an air pocket, and with a small, boxed-end wrench, he bled the line and the motor started up and ran okay, but he said, "Take this wrench with you in case you need it." Being boaters, it didn't seem to be a big problem at the time. Too much confidence maybe, but neither of us had any major concern at this point.

On our way home, we had to go under a Pacific Coast highway bridge, a low one. However, the mast was equipped with a hinge at the deck level to allow it to be lowered in a forward direction. Since neither of us had ever lowered a mast like this before, the dealer went over the process with us very carefully. I printed notes on the large envelope so that we wouldn't miss any important steps. We were instructed to lower it to about thirty degrees, as any lower would make it hard to raise. He made a significant point that we should always maintain control of the backstay so as not to drop the mast! His warning was well noted and understood.

When this training session was over, we were anxious to get this new baby out of the slip and on the way home. However, after motoring out of the marina and outside the Long Beach breakwater, Gunter changed the plan and wanted to put up the sails to test out the boat.

As he desired, we put up the sails without much difficulty, and like many sail boaters, in my experience, Gunter looked for another boat to race, primarily to see how well his boat handled. With a good breeze, the boat performed well, and we enjoyed sailing near other boats and engaging in a little cheerful racing. It was enjoyable, but soon we headed toward home. Before we entered the Seal Beach ammunition depot channel to the harbor, we lowered the jib and mainsail carefully and got the diesel engine going with no thoughts about its performance. Very confident after the sailing venture, we were ready for the next phase of the trip.

Now, our thoughts immediately turned to the tricky maneuver of lowering the mast well before we got to the bridge. So, we got out the big brown envelope with the instructions on it and followed them precisely, feeling pretty good about how we handled it.

Soon our self-satisfaction turned into panic, the diesel engine shut down, but with the wind coming from astern, we were not in immediate danger of hitting the bridge. However, about seventy-five yards past the bridge, the channel turned sharply to the right, and since the wind was pushing us into the direction of the marsh, we had to take action fast! Bleeding the engine did not work this time, our efforts could not get it started.

I told Gunter to get the anchor out while I continued to try getting the motor going and to be ready to drop it to prevent us from going aground in the marsh but, being a new boat, the anchor line was tangled up. We were in a crisis—mistake number three. Being in relatively shallow water, we didn't need much line to help us stop the boat, and we were fortunate enough to untangle enough to get us stopped. We were saved!

When we could breathe again, we asked a passing trailer-boater heading in to ask the harbor patrol to come get us. Fortunately, the harbor patrol office was located next to the boat ramp. In the meantime, we got the mast back up and locked in place. Shortly thereafter, the harbor patrol in the red boat arrived and tied up alongside. After we hauled up the anchor, they proceeded to take us the short distance to Gunter's slip. Embarrassed about our dilemma, we tried to hide our faces so no one saw us limping home undertow. We thanked the harbor patrol for rescuing us and went below to relax, and our bodies needed relaxation, badly.

Exhausted after this harrowing experience but feeling good about our efforts to recover from a near disaster, we opened the chilled bottle of champagne to celebrate ownership of a new boat. A perfect end to another adventurous day, we survived. Wow! Let's not do that again!

PLATTERS TIME

B RANSON, MISSOURI, is a place we don't hear a lot about, but after reading this story, I hope you'll make a trip there; you'll be surprised at what you've missed.

In our planning for the trip, our best source of information turned out to be the internet. My wife's college roommate and her husband, Nancy and John Bowser, planned to join us in Branson. They suggested we purchase tickets for the most popular shows well in advance of our trip for the best seating, which turned out to be excellent advice. We never sat farther from the stage than row ten. Since some of the theaters in Branson are huge, with 2,500 seats or more, we highly recommend getting your tickets ahead of time for the popular evening shows. There was plenty of parking for the shows and ushers conveniently showed everyone to their seats.

Traffic, on the other hand, on the "strip" can be awful at times since Branson is just a small town that grew up very fast around existing infrastructure. The main strip has a traffic light at almost every block, with traffic moving very slowly, but there are parallel back roads that move faster. For our visit in May, we did not en-counter a problem with crowds and traffic because we left to arrive early for the shows. So, make plans accordingly. From our experience, we decided that it would be pure folly to visit Branson during the peak summer period.

Another key consideration for a Branson visit is your flight plan: The nearest airport is in Springfield, about forty miles away where you can rent a car and drive over. Now that the highway construction has been completed, it's four lanes all the way, with directions clearly marked.

Probably one of the first questions that comes to mind is, "How did Branson come to be?" Well, without going into too much detail, it turns out that good fishing had something to do with it along with a series of excellent promoters of the region. Prior to the dams that were erected on the White River to create the popular lakes, people from Kansas City, St. Louis, and the sur-rounding metropolitan areas used to spend the summer on the banks of the river. Many built summer homes, camps, and tourist resorts to take advantage of the moderate summer climate and excellent fishing, boating, and water activities.

The series of dams that were built beginning in 1919 created several lakes. Table Rock Lake, which we fished, is a warm-water lake holding bass, but Lake Taney Como, which receives cold water from the depths of Table Rock, is known for its rainbow and brown trout. What else can you catch? Walleye, striped bass, catfish, crappie, perch, and more were also available.

Anyway, a lot of the country music stars came to the area for the fishing, liked the community, and moved there. Roy Clark was one of the first to arrive. Incidentally, Table Rock Lake is listed as one of the top ten bass-fishing lakes in North America with about 845 miles of shoreline. Several bass tournaments are held there every year. Lake Taney Como is approximately twenty-two miles long and has produced rainbow and brown trout up to twenty-five pounds. Could you handle one of those on a fly rod? Wow!

The Butterfield Overland Mail stage line, established in 1858, brought national attention to Springfield as the departure point for the west. It was twenty-five days to San Francisco, averaging 120 miles a day. Remind me not to complain about airport delays. Residents from Tennessee, Kentucky, and North Carolina migrated to the area in the early nineteenth century, and Springfield was incorporated in 1838. We heard that Wild Bill Hickock killed a man there over a gambling debt in 1865. Osage Indians, who initially called the Ozarks home, were sadly force-marched to Oklahoma in 1838.

There are good restaurants in the area, as you might expect, but I must admit we didn't have a lot of time for "fine" dining. We were on the go every day, and our schedule gave us time for quick meals only. We had a couple of good dinners at a popular chain restaurant. Dinner at the Wooden Nickel, a local family restaurant we enjoyed, was reasonable and tasty. The Pzazz was recommended to us as a luncheon destination, and if you go there, order the prime rib sandwich. It is incredible! This restaurant had a Southern California connection, it was owned by Jack Hamilton, a former pitcher for the Angels. We had a nice conversation with him, and he sent over free desserts for the four of us. Nice touch!

Other than shows and fishing, there are several golf courses, a scenic railway trip (which was enjoyed by Nancy and John during one of our fishing days), Stone Hill Winery (where we sampled and bought some excellent wine), Silver Dollar City (kind of like Knotts Berry Farm in California—life in the old Ozarks), and for fishermen, Bass Pro Shops in Springfield. You'll pass right by it on your way to Branson—it has a thirty-thousand-gallon saltwater aquarium and three hundred thousand square feet of outdoor "stuff." A must-stop place.

As for the music shows, there is something in Branson for everyone. The most popular show in town, while we were there, was Shoji Tabuchi who plays the violin, which may not sound very exciting, but his show was like a Las Vegas variety show. It was spectacular. He had an orchestra composed of about twenty-five graduate musicians that accompany him and other performers in almost any style of music you can name: country, cajun, classical, popular, and Japanese. The show included the most sophisticated laser show in the world, a Japanese dragon parade, and featured the largest drum in the world, which took twenty years to make—it also required the stage to be reinforced. Like Las Vegas, there were constant costume changes to go with the musical mood swings. Shoji's theater seated 2,500 and was sold out twice a day. If my memory is correct, the show changed every six weeks.

There were over forty music shows going on during our visit, and since we fished for two days, we had to make some tough decisions on which shows to attend. We thoroughly enjoyed all of those we attended. For the evening shows besides Shoji, we saw Mickey Gilly, the Oak Ridge Boys, and the Platters. The Oaks were playing at the Grand Palace, where the Miss USA Pageant was held along with most of the televised events coming out of Branson—it seated over three thousand, and featured a changing schedule of big-name stars. We went to two morning shows, Barbara Fairchild and Jim Owen, and one afternoon show, The Sons of the Pioneers. As mentioned, they were great and very informal. For example, when we walked into the lobby for the Jim Owen show, he was there with a cup of coffee talking with the people as they arrived. we talked with him and took pictures of him with our wives. That's typical; most of the performers came down from the stage at intermission and after the show to sign autographs and talk with you. It's kind of like talking with a good neighbor, real friendly. Jim Owen had been in nine movies, a couple as Hank Williams and one in which he played a bad guy that gets beaten up by Sonny Bono—how humiliating could that have been? He was not only a good singer, but also an excellent comedian. It was a good show.

The Sons of the Pioneers trace their heritage back to Roy Rogers (née Leonard Sly) who formed the group and even after leaving them for the movies, featured them in many of his movies. Many of the songs featured in their show were written by members of the group, including "Cool Water" and "Tumbling Tumbleweeds," and several members gained some degree of fame in the movies and TV like Pat Brady, Roy's TV sidekick, and Ken Curtis as Festus on *Gunsmoke*. It was fun learning facts about various groups and individual performers that we had listened to for years.

We stayed at Grand Vista's Branson Yacht Club, a time-share, just a couple of miles out of town and very convenient to the shows and fishing. The marina there, Table Rock Marina, includes a bait and tackle shop where you can also rent boats. Prior to our visit, they put us in touch with a great, young, professional bass fisherman, Ryan Sifford, who was sponsored by two popular boat companies. We were lucky to catch Ryan in town, and what a pleasure he was to fish with.

On our first day, we left the marina dock at 7:00 a.m., a two-minute drive from our condo, and caught our first bass less than an hour later. It was a Kentucky Bass; very similar looking to a largemouth but unlike the largemouth, the jaw does not extend beyond the eye. We were using green pumpkin colored plastic worms rigged Carolina style with eight pound test line, and they worked great!

We moved around the lake and caught and released large-mouth, Kentucky, and the prized smallmouth bass. As we talked during the day, we found out that Ryan had fished with Jimmy Houston, Hank Parker, Mel Tillis—who makes his home in Branson—Roy Clark, and many other well-known celebrities. Ryan was always checking to make sure we were having fun, and we were.

While moving around, we saw lots of wildlife: blue herons, turtles, hawks, Canada geese, and many birds. It's not unusual to see deer, wild pigs, and things of that nature we were told, and one thing I haven't mentioned is how beautiful this area was, so green and relatively little development, but there were some incredibly beautiful homes up to forty thousand square feet. Hard to believe!

On our second day of fishing, we began using topwater with redfin jointed minnow plugs with a horsetail on the hook. We caught and released a few bass before we returned to our trusty worm rigs which seemed to work a little better for us. A few weeks earlier during the spring spawn, top-water rigs worked great. So, if that's your thing, time your trip for late April—that should work out. For us, it couldn't have been better, we caught and released lots of fish, and found a great fishing guide who was a lot of fun to spend a few days with. We're going back to Table Rock, for sure.

On our last day in Branson, we decided to go to an afternoon show, eat an early dinner, and then go back to our condo to pack up. Our friends, the Bowsers, had a two-day drive to Houston and planned to leave early the next morning. So, after the show, we went to the chain restaurant again for dinner and, after eating, John and I went out to the porch for a little rocking chair time while our wives were shopping in the country store.

Shortly afterward, two men came out the door, one of them with a dozen or more gold chains around his neck remarked, "Why don't we play a game of checkers before we leave?"

At that point, I jumped up out of my rocking chair and said, "Why don't you take my chair, there's a checkerboard right here." Then I noticed that one of the men had a white cane with a red tip on the end of it. Looked crazy to me, and I remarked, "How can you have competition with him? Sure looks unfair to me, and I have to referee this checker game."

As we talked, Nancy came out the door and asked me if I knew who these men were. When I said no, I have no idea. She said, "These guys are the Platters." When I was young, we loved to dance to their music; this was a thrill! They asked, have you seen our show. "No," we said. They insisted that we come that night as their guests—VIP seating! I told Rooster, the leader of the group, that we had to go back to our place and pack to get ready to leave early in the morning. He insisted though, and reluctantly, we agreed to go to their show. He told us to wait for fifteen minutes before we left the restaurant to give him time to arrange the tickets for us at the "will call" window.

When we arrived at the theater, he was still at the window. When he left, we picked up our tickets and went inside where the usher escorted us down to our seats. Guess where? Very front seats, of course!

The music was to die for! The show included all their great hits, "Twilight Time," "The Great Pretender," "My Prayer," "You'll Never Know," "Smoke gets In Your Eyes," "Magic Touch," and my favorite, "Only You." At the end of the show, our host, Lawrence "Rooster" Randell, came down from the stage, and gave Nancy and Pat a long-stemmed rose, and danced with Pat in the aisle. That was a magical moment for the four of us, a once-in-a-lifetime experience, but that experience wasn't over yet. There was more to come that night.

After the show, the Platters invited the audience to meet them in the lobby for photos and autographs. Obviously, there was a dilemma for us, it was great sitting up front, but getting out would be a challenge with the huge crowd ahead of us. By the time we reached the lobby from our front row seats, the line would be a mile long. About that time, we saw an exit light over a door next to the stage, no one was using it or guarding it.

Our wives said "We can't wait, let's go out that door," and we went out the side door. Guess who was coming up the sidewalk? Rooster, and he said, "Where are you going?"

I said, "Rooster, we have to get back and pack, that line upfront will go around the building."

Rooster said, "Don't worry about the line," took Pat by the arm and started up the sidewalk.

At that point, I turned to John and said, "I guess we're going up front." We followed Rooster, who had Pat, and went back into the lobby for autographs and photos of our new friends, The Platters, Lawrence Randell, Eddie Stoval, Walter White (who likes to fish), Willie Nash, and the beautiful, sweet Dee Dee Hamilton. What a way to end a wonderful week in Branson! Wow, double wow!

Branson is an awesome place that doesn't get a lot of hype, but I hope you'll include it in your vacation plans someday. I promise you'll have a trip to remember. It sure has special memories for us.

Pat with her friends, the Platters. L–R: Lawrence
"Rooster" Randell, Willie Nash, Pat, and Walter White.

PIRATE

O UR FRIENDS FROM CALIFORNIA, Wes and Betty, joined us for a week's visit to Jekyll Island, Georgia, along with Jack Robertson and his friend Theo, our daughter Pam, and granddaughter Jennifer. We had rented a five-bedroom house on the beach, as we had done on previous trips to the area, and sharing coastal Georgia was always a joy for us. We think they met most of the local Paulk clan while we were there. During visits to the millionaires' old mansions on Jekyll Island, they learned where the federal reserve was born behind closed doors in the hotel there.

Later, on St. Simon's Island, we toured the ruins of Fort Fredericka where they learned about the Battle of Bloody Marsh which was instrumental in keeping the Spanish out of Georgia. Jim's sister, Dorothy, arranged a tour of Christ Church, built in 1884, and where several VIPs have been married including Vice President Alben Barkley and Sara Churchill, not to each other. Another item of interest, we were told that John Wesley, who founded the Methodist Church, preached under the beautiful live oak trees on the grounds there.

During the tour of the Jekyll Island homes of Rockefeller, Crane, Goodrich, and other wealthy members of the Jekyll Island Club, we learned about the former owners of the island who sold it to the United States after World War II. I stayed with the car after dropping them off and headed for the parking lot.

As I parked the car in the lot, I saw a shrimp boat pull up to the dock and drop someone off. I didn't pay much attention after that, but as I got out and locked the car, a man walked up. It was clear that he hadn't shaved in a couple of weeks, his clothes were filthy, and several of his front teeth were missing.

He said, "Hi, do you know where I can get a taxi?"

I replied, "I'm sorry, but there are no taxis on Jekyll Island, where do you want to go?"

Now the man—who looked like a homeless person to me—said, "I'm off the shrimp boat out there in the river, and we wanted to buy a bottle of bourbon to go with dinner after we anchor the boat."

"Hop in, there is a package store at the strip center a couple of miles from here, no problem." As we drove to the liquor store, I asked him how the fishing was going. His reply was, "awful, very few shrimp in 4 days of fishing." They were about to give up and head for home in Florida. When we got back to the parking area, I dropped him off at the head of the dock. He asked me to wait a minute, don't drive off, and I watched as the boat pulled up to the dock for him to reboard. He didn't get on board, but instead, came back to the car with a bag, and thanked me again for helping them. When I looked inside, it contained several pounds of shrimp, maybe their entire catch? I had tears in my eyes by the time our group returned to the car. Our Houston gal, Miss Betty, boiled shrimp for dinner that evening, sho' was good.

Wes commented, "When I saw that pirate-looking guy get in your car, I was sure that he was going to slit your throat!" For me, I never felt better for having done a good deed even if my guests were terrified! I had created a beautiful evening for the crew of that shrimp boat.

Shrimp boat—"pirate" ship.

SAVED BY ORVILLE

SOME OF YOU MAY KNOW that we've published articles on fishing, and that all fishermen have a way of exaggerating and embellishing stories. Please keep this in mind as this story unfolds. Remember that I'm just a farmer from Georgia, and I'm not used to all of you city folk and your strange goings-on. Orville— yes, you must know with that name—is from Oklahoma. Wes is from Texas, and they were bound to meet someday and go into business together, well, maybe that's not what it should be called. Maybe it was Wes making Orville rich!

I'm getting a little ahead of myself. So, let's step back and start from the beginning. Wes called me, "I'm thinking about trading in my RV and getting a thirty-two-foot Bluebird that I saw advertised down at RV World off the five Freeway. How 'bout you and Pat go with us to look at it, and help me negotiate this deal if it looks like it'll work out."

"Okay, Wes, let's go. But there is nothing wrong with the RV that you have."

An observation, Wes was never happy unless he was buying

more or exchanging rolling stock! I won't list all of it, but believe me, he has more equipment and cars than most farmers and used car lots.

At RV World, we found the dealer and a very eager car dealer with money wheels turning in his eyeball sockets. He was, immediately, our best friend when Wes mentioned the ad for the thirty-two-foot RV. Our car dealer broke out his key, we went aboard, and proceeded to inspect every nook and cranny. Betty and Pat checked out the kitchen appliances while we asked about the engine (an important subject to be discussed later), the generator, and sundry other questions, not nearly as important as the engine—a diesel, about the best there is. The RV was built in Georgia which automatically won approval from me (a Georgia boy).

After the check-out was done, Wes and I sat down with the car dealer in the bow—that is, the front of the BUS—to do some big-time negotiating. Betty and Pat likely said a quick prayer for the poor salesman and sat down in the galley area to talk, something they both received A-pluses in throughout their school years. As I remember it, we got down to a very low price, and like all good salesmen, he said, "Let me run this by my manager, I don't think he's going to like it."

So, he bebops off the RV and disappears for quite a while. "Nope," he says, "We can't do this deal at that price."

I asked, "How long has this been on the market?"

He answered, "A year."

Next question, "Okay, now let's calculate how much your carrying costs will be if you carry it in your inventory for another year."

Off he goes to talk with the unseen manager, and when he comes back, he said, "The deal was approved."

Now a subject that had not been in the conversation. "Okay, now how about the trade-in value of our current RV?" We could tell when he went back to see the boss again, he expected to be fired or worse. They gave Wes credit on the trade-in, and were very happy to see us leave their place before we brought up anything else!

With the deal finally consummated, the trade was made, and Wes picked up his beautiful, fully equipped, thirty-two-foot Bluebird a few days later. Is this a shaggy dog story or what? Life with Wes was just like that!

Sometime later, Wes called, "Have you ever been to Lake Isabella?" When I said no, he replied, "We have a holiday weekend coming up, [remember holiday weekend], let's go up there to try out this wonderful, luxurious motor home and do a little fishing. The trout average twenty-five pounds plus or minus." Maybe minus a lot, but "fishing" was the keyword.

"Okay, let's go." Preparations began at once to make this trip a *memorable* one—remember that word too.

We got on the road on Friday and headed north to Bakersville, home of Buck Owens, and oil-drilling roughnecks from Oklahoma. What a nice, smooth ride, everything was going great when we turned off the freeway and headed toward the road that would take us up the mountain to the lake. Suddenly there was a very loud bang of something big hitting the bottom of the coach. It was like hitting a land mine, get the idea? Wes pulled off the road immediately. Then we crawled under the carriage, checked the engine, looked back on the road to see if we'd hit something big.

Nothing, we saw nothing. Wes said, "Let's go on, but keep a close eye and ear tuned in for further indications of problems." So, up the narrow, two-lane, mountain road we went in the thirty-two-foot RV. We couldn't help but notice that the left-hand side of the road dropped off, maybe a mile—or looked that way anyhow. Soon, with all of us sweating it out, an announcement comes from our driver, Wes Bannister, "The TEMPERATURE is starting to rise."

"No problem, let's turn off the A/C, refrigerator, everything that might weigh on the cooling system." I said. We did that. No luck, the temp was still going up. No choice, we must go down the hill.

Now, understand, there is virtually no place to get off the road and turn around, and we were between two curves. "Wes, I'll walk up to the uphill curve to stop downhill traffic. Pat, you walk downhill to stop uphill traffic." Wes, with encouragement and cheerleading from Betty, commenced turning that sucker around with very little room to do so. Our Texas boy, trained on turning trucks around on muddy roads, got the job done without going over the cliff. Boy, that was a close call, it seemed to take forever, too.

Wes, old buddy, old pal, we can coast down this hill, I'm thinking. And he did, using the brakes sparingly. Then I remembered, "I had seen a big CAT sign outside Bakersville, but looking at my watch to determine if they might still be open—this WAS a holiday weekend—and what if they left work early?

Now, we we're sweating big time. What if we couldn't find the CAT dealer again? Mile after mile, we looked for the sign, and glory be, we found it. With our pulse rate at moon level, and a little strategic maneuvering, we found our way to the garage area with huge doors that could accommodate an eighteen-wheeler. Hallelujah, the doors were open too! We could breathe again! We were just in time.

"Wes, meet Orville, my friend. He now owns your butt, get used to it!" Orville was the manager of the garage and our rescuer of the day.

After a quick look at the engine, he found that an idling sprocket for the fan belt had broken in half, bounced on the road, and hit the undercarriage hard. No spare, but he could get one next week. Orville and Wes fell in love, and Wes left the RV there for Orville to check, replace, and upgrade everything for umpteen gazillion bucks. "Come back and get it in a month," he said.

What about us hitch-hikers (that's us)? Almost, anyway. We arranged for a rental car, and Orville gave us directions to a nearby, "nice" motel. However, when we arrived at the motel, the first thing we noticed was that it had no door leading to a lobby and check-in desk. Upon further examination, there was, in fact, a window with bullet-proof glass in it and one of those drawers for the big money transaction between the office and the sidewalk.

By this time, we were mentally and physically exhausted, too much so, to go looking for another place to stay. This was as good a place to die as any other. Yep, there had to be danger nearby, we had dinner at a fast-food place, went to bed, and drove back to Huntington Beach in the rental car, just happy we survived. What an adventure, and we found Orville, a name that I'll never forget.

By the way, we have yet to make it to Lake Isabella. Wes, ole buddy, ole pal, you were one of a kind, and even though you were Army, and I was Navy, I've never had a better friend. Unfortunately, we lost Wes a few years ago, RIP, I sure miss you.

Camper—Betty Bannister, Pat, and Wes Bannister at their camper.
Betty was Pat's "Little Bitty Buddy."

Z-WAT, A SAILFISH MECCA

O N OUR TRIP DOWN, to the Ixtapa-Zihuatanejo (Z-Wat), Mexico, area in 1999, we flew down from Los Angeles by way of Mexico City, and after a long delay there, we vowed to do everything we could to avoid this itinerary in the future. What had started out as a routine trip had turned into one of those all-day expeditions that every traveler abhors. Missing the cocktail hour was a bummer! Our advice is to look at nonstop flights from Los Angeles to Z-Wat.

This was an especially exciting trip because, all together, we had three other couples meeting us from the east coast, Mike and Nancy Reu from Camden, South Carolina; my brother and his wife, Bobby and Vila Paulk, from St. Mary's, Georgia; and Vila's sister and her husband, Cathy and Tommy Egbert, also from St. Mary's. Joining Pat and me on our flight down were Bud and Marcene Galli, our neighbors in Huntington Beach. None of the four guys had ever caught a sailfish before—so, you can guess what our goal was: we wanted each of them to catch at least one sailfish. This was going to be exciting!

If you have read previous articles we have written about our Z-Wat trips, you know this is one of our favorite places in the world. For fishing arrangements, we have always received top-notch care from Larry Edwards of Cortez Yacht Charters. He can fix you up with a panga or a cruiser. A bit of advice we can't emphasize enough, you need to book your fishing trips with someone you can trust, like Larry. Perhaps the biggest rip-off on Mexico trips is paying in advance for fishing trips that disappear on you. You arrive at the dock in the morning to find there is no boat with the name you have chartered for the day.

For our trip, Larry had arranged two trips on the *Vamanos Dos*, a thirty-three-foot boat, out of Puerto Mio in Zihuatanejo. It is powered by twin diesels that move the boat along at fifteen to twenty knots. A wide cockpit made it a very comfortable boat from which to fish, and even with five men on board, it didn't seem crowded.

Each time we visited Ixtapa, we were amazed at the improvements that had been made since our previous trip. It was developed specifically as a tourist resort to complement the old town of Zihuatanejo, located just three and a half miles away. Fonatur, the Mexican tourist development bureau, has the responsibility and the resources to do the infrastructure work and to encourage the expansion of tourist facilities. And while we aren't seeing a lot of new hotels/restaurants, the roads and parkways are more beautiful each visit.

Some of our gang took a city tour and returned with not only a little history about the area, but a better understanding of the opportunities available to visitors. For example, according to the guide, Zihuatanejo means "land of the beautiful women." That should grab your attention! It seems that many years ago all men had been captured and used as slaves and for human sacrifice by the bloodthirsty Aztecs. Wow! Glad we didn't visit in those days.

Also, we learned that around 1844, sailing ships arriving in the area from the south Pacific brought coconuts and started a very large coconut plantation. Nowadays, everywhere you look, you see coconut palms, and if you travel north by boat, there are miles and miles of palms at the beach line—looks like a South Seas Island. It is truly a beautiful area. We are told that 90 percent of the visitors to Ixtapa are the affluent of Mexico City, and you don't see a lot of Norte Americanos, and that's not all bad.

The night before our first scheduled fishing trip, we made our sandwiches, set our alarms, arranged for two cabs, and went to bed early. Our "first-timers" were excited, and we knew that several of them would be so excited, they would have trouble sleeping. The next morning, we were up early, and after a quick bowl of cereal and a cup of coffee, we went downstairs to await our cabs. Shortly, they were there, and we were on our way over to the municipal pier in Zihuatanejo when it was still dark outside.

At the pier, there was some activity, but it wasn't anything like the madness you encounter at the pier in Cabo San Lucas. It appeared that only six or seven boats were preparing to go out, and there was little to no congestion in the harbor. In no time we found our boat, *Vamanos Dos*, and her captain, Jaime Morales, and his mate, Carlos. The boat was running, and as soon as we got on board, we were underway. Blue water was only a few miles out, and the boat's diesel engines sounded great. On the way out, Carlos prepared a dozen frozen mullets for trolling baits and set up the rods in the ready position. Thirty minutes after leaving the pier, we were fishing.

Since we had five fishermen, we set up a rotation schedule by drawing numbers from a hat. Mike Reu, who had very little prior fishing experience was first up, and barely ten minutes after the baits went in the water, Mike was in the chair hooked up and huffing and puffing as he practiced all the directions coming his way. But like a seasoned pro, he soon had the fish at the boat. Unfortunately, the hook was too deep, and the fish was bleeding profusely. This turned out to be the only sailfish that was boated during our two days of fishing. Mike was a happy camper after catching the biggest fish of his life, and the most impressive one.

There was a slight wind chop and no white caps, a beautiful cloudless day as we got the bait back in the water and began trolling again. As I looked around the boat, everyone was smiling. It was obvious they now were "believers." Five minutes later, our second sail was on, and our next angler, Tommy Egbert, was ready. Only ten minutes later, his fish was at the boat, and we watched as the fish was released and swam away unharmed. We were only six miles out of Z-Wat.

Our next fisherman had to wait fifteen minutes before it was his turn, but Bud knew what to do. He had caught his first marlin earlier in the year in Kauai, and after only six minutes, his fish was released. All these fish probably weighed around one hundred pounds.

Six minutes after Bud caught his fish, Jim was hooked up. It was a big fish that seemed to jump a couple of times a minute. After a fight for six minutes, the fish was released to fight another day. It was now only 9:30, and we were seven miles offshore with a count of four sailfish. Now, where else can you catch four billfish in just a few hours?

We had another knockdown by a dorado at noon, but it didn't stick. Bobby, our last angler, had been up for hours with no luck, and it was apparent to the rest of us that he must have been a jinx—he was catching a lot of flak, not fish. We got back in around 2:00 and caught a couple of cabs waiting at the pier. Arriving back at our condos, we had some great stories to tell—except for Bobby, who was the butt of a lot of jokes! He took it well though, and he'd be up first on the next trip.

A couple of days later, we were up early to catch our cabs over to Z-Wat. Our crew on the *Vamanos Dos* would be different because Jaime was ill. So, his brother, Efrain, with his mate, Jesus, would take care of us for the day. Jesus sewed the hooks up inside the mullets on our way out, and just like the last trip, the boat soon slowed down, and the baits were in the water. Birds and porpoises were abundant in this area only six or seven miles out. The sun was just coming up and the conditions looked great. We had five baits in the water, two on the outriggers, two on the Z-wing downriggers, and one down the middle. We were ready.

Twenty minutes later, a sailfish hit the starboard rigger, jumped once, and was gone. Oh boy, Bobby's jinx was still with us. Fifteen minutes later we missed a hit again on the starboard rigger, and then on each downrigger. Four hits and nada! Bobby was being kidded mercilessly. Fifteen minutes later, he had a chance to redeem himself as the sail took the port Z-Wing down planner. After he got the fish to the boat and it was released, everyone patted him on the back, and thanked him for getting the skunk off the boat. He was all smiles after catching his first billfish.

A half-hour later, Tommy caught a sail that hit on the bait, fished down the middle, and had it to the boat in five minutes. He did a nice job and was all smiles as he released his fish. Fifteen minutes later, Jim was on as the sail hit the starboard rigger. The fish was a nice one and was released after a fight of about ten minutes. Eight minutes later, Bud became our hero by catching a fifteen to twenty-pound dorado we desperately wanted for dinner that night.

An hour later, a sail hit the port Z-Wing and then the starboard one, jumped once and was gone. An hour later, another sail hit the port Z-Wing, took the bait, and said bye-bye. Boy, had we missed a bunch of fish!

Finally, Mike hooked up again with a big fish, and after a fight of about twenty minutes, let it go to fight again another day. At one o'clock, we headed in, and everyone was all smiles again as we laughed about our count for the day, four sails, one dorado, and five other chances. We were a happy group. After catching two sails, Mike indicated that he was starting to like fishing.

On the way in, Jesus filleted our dorado that we later took to the El Faro restaurant. The chef did a fabulous job and our gang of ten gave thanks to our hero, Bud, for providing us with such a great meal.

In two days of fishing, we had raised thirteen billfish and caught eight, not unusual fishing for this area. Why? There is virtually no commercial fishing in the area—only a few pangas who go out daily to catch bottom fish with handlines for the local restaurants, and the few sport boats who go out have been releasing their fish for years. In other words, the fishing pressure is not there as it is in so many of the other Mexican resorts.

FISHING IN THE GRAVEYARD

―――――

Y EP! There really is a place where you can fish for largemouth bass in a graveyard and catch them too. The lake is named El Salto for the nearby town.

Obviously, there is a story behind this fishing experience. In the past thirty or forty years, as you may be aware, there has been a lot of development in Mexico—resort towns, golf courses, and new fishing resorts. Tourism is one of the largest industries in Mexico, and each time you visit, more has been done to improve the tourist experience. As a result of the growth, additional municipal services have been required.

There was (and still is) a small village named El Salto (The Jump) that happened to be located where a new dam and the resulting reservoir were planned. It would provide water for the nearby agricultural areas and a new supply of badly needed electricity. In the early 1980s, the government went to the people of the village, who had homes and had lived there for generations, and told them the town would have to be relocated. Each family would be provided a new home and free land for farming; the graveyard would have to be relocated, and a new church would be built for them.

However, some of the gravestones were too large or heavy to be relocated to the new cemetery and, consequently, were left in place. While we were there, the tops of these gravestones were partially out of the water. That's the way it works in Mexico, and the government owns the churches.

By 1985, the town of El Salto had been relocated nearby, a new dam had been constructed, and the reservoir was being filled. Florida-strain largemouth bass were added to bring additional tourists to the area, and a great new bass fishing destination was created—one of the best in the world. When full, this lake will be sixteen miles long and has been designated as an ecological reserve to keep its resources from being exploited. During a day's fishing experience, one will view a wide variety of wildlife, including herons, otters, owls, hawks, vultures, deer, and so much more. It is a beautiful area with trees, cacti, small rocky islands, and areas of water hyacinths. The lake-record bass hangs over the bar at the new Anglers Inn resort on the lake, and it weighed in at an impressive 18.8 pounds. Who caught it? The well-known tour-nament bass angler, Kevin Van Dam.

Now, where is this lake and how do you get there? Pat and I flew down to Mazatlán at the end of April, primarily to fish off-shore, but after a fruitless day of looking for tuna and sailfish, we decided that if we wanted to catch anything during our visit, we were going to need a "plan B." Clearly, plan A was not going to be a productive one. Prior to our trip, our research turned up this new bass lake and, from everything that we had heard, it had begun to produce a lot of bass. As an old bass fisherman from Georgia, this kind of fishing was like a trip home for me. The new lake is in the mountain foothills, seventy-seven miles north of Mazatlán, and reached by an easy, one-and-a-half-hour drive on mostly toll roads.

Before going into the specifics of our day of fishing El Salto, let me tell you a little about Mazatlán. It is a busy port city with no rain from the end of October to June, and is about two hundred miles north of Puerto Vallarta on the Pacific coast of mainland Mexico. It is about the same latitude as Hawaii. The airport is twenty miles south of the city, and there is a daily train and bus service from Nogales, 720 miles to the north. A ferry to La Paz is the primary means of supplying goods to Baja California, including Pacifico beer made in Mazatlán. Try it, you'll like it.

The city of five hundred thousand people has the largest shrimp boat fleet in Mexico of seventy-five thousand boats, mostly outboard motor-powered, that supply nine different plants that process more than forty thousand tons of shrimp annually. It's the shrimp capital of the world—most of which is shipped frozen to the US. One of the largest tuna canning factories on the west coast is also located there and is supplied by a fleet that goes as far south as Panama.

The sportfishing boats are in eight different charter company fleets with the best season for sailfish in the May–November period (maybe we were too early), and marlin November–May (maybe we were too late). The largest marlin to date is a 412-pound blue, while a nine hundred-pound black was caught nearby after a seven-hour fight (maybe a good reason to stay away).

As for other things to do, hunting for waterfowl, dove, quail, pheasant, deer, wild boar, and mountain lions is available in the nearby hills; there are tennis courts, eighteen-hole golf courses—including one designed by Lee Trevino and one by Robert Trent Jones Jr.—about ten miles from the airport.

A couple of suggestions—since the airport is quite a distance from town, it is best to arrange for transportation to and from the airport by shuttle bus *prior* to your arrival. Otherwise, it can be a hassle and expensive to do at the airport. Also, we found that the peso exchange rate was better in Mazatlán than in the US. As for places to eat, our favorite was La Costa Marinera, right on the beach, they had great seafood, reasonable, and there was a great opera singer providing the entertainment for a mostly local crowd on Saturday night. We saw no one leave while we were there. It was just a short walk for us on the beach from our hotel, Pueblo Bonito. For Italian food, Angelo's—adjacent to the Pueblo Bonito—was good, and for Tex-Mex, try La Casa Country for a mixed crowd of locals and tourists (it can be noisy). Senor Frogs is more for drinking than dinner; one drink, enjoy the show, three drinks, you *are* the show. Look out for the tequila drinking contests!

On the day we went to El Salto, our guide, Honorato (Hono) Elizalde, picked us up at our hotel at 5:00 a.m. for the trip to the lake. After spending so much time traveling the roads in Baja California over the years, we were surprised to see how nice the toll roads were. As an aside, it was interesting to learn that mechanics provide free service to travelers with car problems on the toll roads in Mexico. At our last toll booth, we stopped briefly to use the restrooms since there were none available when we visited the lake.

We arrived at the lake a little after 6:30 a.m. and quickly got the boat loaded. Surprisingly, we found it pulled up on the bank and tied to a tree, don't laugh. Nearby, there were three other boats and most of them belonged to Hono. Within ten minutes of arriving at the lake, we had caught and released our first bass. The lake is full of trees and cacti, and I believe there is a bass or two at each one.

We used plastic worms rigged Texas-style to avoid too many snags and, yes, we fished up in the trees occasionally, but didn't spend a lot of time pulling on bushes and I don't think we lost a lure all day. Fishing under the water hyacinth areas reminded me of fishing in Georgia and Florida, while bouncing the worms off the rock-sided islands reminded me of fishing in Indiana. During the day, we saw houses, gravestones, and all kinds of structures that were partially underwater. It did feel strange casting worms at the gravestones, but fish were there. We fished until noon and caught fish the entire time, twenty-five to thirty each, were caught and released, and we had shots at more. Needless to say, we had a wonderful time, and by the time we returned to the hotel, we felt like Hono was a member of our family. He was a real professional and spoke excellent English. He has now built a very nice lodge at the lake, Anglers Inn, and his wife has an office at the Pueblo Bonita in Mazatlán and can help you arrange your bass fishing tour—all equipment is provided, or you may bring your own. As an aside, it took him several years to obtain permits and to build the resort on the lake, but feedback from friends that have been there more recently has been very positive.

There are several fishing clubs that contract with Hono to hold annual bass tournaments at the lake also—so, this might be an idea for your club to consider. One thing about this lake from what we've heard and experienced, you always catch fish. Try El Salto, you'll love it. Fishing in the graveyard is a real kick!

NAVY

D URING MY CHILDHOOD, I was into hunting, fishing, and playing outside with my neighbors and friends during the Great Depression and World War II years. However, when I got to high school, my friends started talking about the future and college and that stimulated my thinking about it as well. Georgia Tech was the primary choice for most of my closest friends and a possibility for me too. However, I can't remember why my dream began about going to the United States Naval Academy in Annapolis, but it became an overwhelming desire. Fortunately, I did not get in after high school graduation because I later learned I was too immature and too ill-prepared at the time for the challenge it would pose for me to go there directly out of high school.

So, I went to North Georgia College in Dahlonega, located in the mountains of north Georgia, where others from my high school had gone to prepare for obtaining entrance to Annapolis. It was a small, full-time military school with good academic programs. There, we were even given an M1 Garand rifle to keep in our room with the requirement to memorize our rifle number and learn to break it down and put it back together blindfolded. Our uniforms were not fancy, but with lots of starch in our shirts, we were often complimented for the way we looked in them. These uniforms were helpful for us when hitch-hiking down the mountains to Atlanta for a Georgia Tech football game with my friends there.

After my first year at North Georgia, I did not get into Annapolis, but a good friend and high school classmate, Carl Croft, who also attended North Georgia, received his appointment to West Point—his dream. So, back to North Georgia for another year, with a promotion in rank and honored with an assignment to Blue Ridge Rifles, a demonstration marching unit, I was fully indoctrinated for any military school.

Things did not look good for an appointment to Annapolis, but after my second year there, I was playing in a golf tournament somewhere in Georgia when a golfing buddy came running to find me. He said my mother had called and that I needed to call her and get home fast.

I had my appointment, but first, I had to pass a rigorous physical exam at the Navy Base in Jacksonville. The eye examination was a problem for many, but not me. I had good eyes, developed during my years of hunting and learning to pick up any movement in the woods. There were strict height and weight requirements, and we had to demonstrate our ability to meet minimum numbers of pushups, pullups, and other exercises. As active as I was at the time, I had no trouble with athletic requirements. I passed and was on my way to Annapolis a week later. Not much time to get ready, but we didn't need to take much with us; in fact, we would be given a box to ship all our clothes home. Everything we needed would be provided.

When I arrived at the Academy, people came from all over the country, no one knew anyone else. So, when time permitted, we were eager to learn about each other, the first thing in our relationship growth. I was so impressed with the background of those around me, valedictorians and presidents of their class, captain of their high school football team, years spent at prestigious universities, and me? I was none of those things, I was average. But soon, I learned that my two years at Dahlonega allowed me to mature and fit right in with everything thrown at us so quickly. The military stuff was easy, I knew how to drill and march, and commands were not new to me while others struggled a bit learning those things.

We were running all summer, constantly changing uniforms for the next activity: swimming, running the obstacle course, rifle range, racing whaleboats on the Severn River, marching everywhere, meals seemed rushed, lots of physical exercises, and everything was recorded. I told friends I had to plan two hours ahead to find time to go to the bathroom. One of my roommates that summer, Alan, had completed three years at the University of Texas, and in his senior year, he was scheduled to be the head cheerleader for football games and editor of their annual. Now, he was starting all over again. My other roommate, John, had attended the University of Arkansas for a year.

Two months later, the upper classes arrived after their midshipman cruise and thirty days of vacation, and our world became even more intense. We hugged the walls as we chopped up the stairs, walked at attention, and even sat at attention on only three inches of our chairs during meals. Being watched closely by seemingly everyone, we were put on report for any rule violations and then spent time on extra duty, marching on the drill field. Those who lacked swimming ability had extra duty in the pool. During the summer we were exposed to every athletic team at Navy: crew, boxing, track and field, gymnastics, fencing, all sports really. Some found sports they had talent in and pursued them during their time at Annapolis.

My best sport was tennis, and I played on the team during competitions with mostly prep schools. After plebe year, I was on the team but never played in matches, clearly outclassed. Al Senior (a classmate) and I won the intramural tennis championship for which Commander Nash, our battalion officer, presented me with a ceramic cup in front of my company because we won points in the annual competition between the six battalions that made up the brigade. This was an unexpected fun event for all of those assembled there, a singular event he made for me.

Going to Annapolis was a dream come true even if we had to endure the rigorous and very challenging plebe year. Academics were hard every year because, unlike a normal university when study time was almost unlimited, at Annapolis, time for study *was* limited, and we lost many classmates who couldn't keep up and bilged out. Math was difficult for some, but not me, I had gone through differential equations at North Georgia, and it was my best subject.

Life for me and most of my classmates fulfilled a dream, and we loved it. The reason my going to Annapolis was so important in my life was that it led me to my wife to be, no question my greatest honor in life was to be married to Pat Metzler. I would never have met her had I not attended the Naval Academy. This story is fully outlined in My Love Story.

After graduation, I attended landing craft control school before reporting to the troop transport *USS Montrose* (APA 212), where I was made third division officer. My men worked in the aft end of the ship and were competent in loading and launching landing craft with our cranes. We also had three landing craft as a maintenance responsibility.

During my ten months in Montrose, we took a battalion of Marines on our ship (with Marines in other ships) in our small fleet to Kodiak Island, off the coast of Alaska, for a practice landing exercise. I had a two-and-a-half-month yard overhaul in Portland, Oregon, and stood junior officer of the watch on the bridge while underway.

When my request for submarine duty was approved, we were off to New London, Connecticut, and Pat started counting the number of moves in our life. Four already in our first year of marriage. Life was an adventure for us indeed.

At Submarine School, we had academic as well as practice exercises to prepare us for assignments to diesel-powered boats. There were no nuclear-powered submarines available to us for assignment. At the mock-up diving stations at the school, we rotated among the various dive stations to not only learn the diving officer procedure, but how to perform the duties at all stations in the control room. We then went out on boats stationed in New London to practice diving and, the important thing, surfacing. The number of dives better equal the number of surfaces. By tradition, submarines are called "boats" in the US Navy.

All aspects of operating a submarine had been taught to us because when we reported aboard our submarine with a limited number of officers on board, we would be assigned to a specific position with extra duties as well.

When we arrived in New London, we were fortunate to get into the limited officer's quarters on the base because Pat was pregnant at the time. Other nonpregnant couples had to find apartments in town. Not only were we within walking distance to almost everything on the base, but glory be, the golf course was across the street, and Pat became the only pregnant caddie on the course—she pulled my golf cart.

Then a major event in our lives took place. After we took Pat to the hospital in New London where she spent twenty hours in labor, our beautiful little girl Pam joined our family. She immediately became the center focus of our lives. With a new baby and free golf across the street, my studies were likely affected, but we graduated and were soon on our way to Norfolk, Virginia, to find our new boat, *USS Redfin* (SSR 272), which had an impressive World War II record. It would be my other home for the next three-and-a-half years.

I was made Electronics Officer with responsibility for the radar and sonar operations and as an additional duty, I had responsibility for classified publications—secret ones. My good friend, and sixth-company Annapolis classmate, Bob Grigsby, was assigned to *Redfin* too. He and his wife, Barbara, lived in an apartment next door to us which was very special since they had a new baby too. With our limited funds, we played bridge often, and our wives did their grocery shopping together.

Our Skipper was Duke Duquette, a full commander who survived frogman duty at Normandy Beach during the major World War II operation, where he and others destroyed obstacles so the landing craft could reach the beach safely. He was an impressive officer and highly decorated, of course. A very high percentage of the frogmen were killed while on their mission to destroy the obstacles. The fact that he survived was a miracle.

Our boat soon departed for a frigid Canada for exercises with Canadian anti-submarine warfare units, where there were times we could not see the bow because of thick snow conditions in water so rough, it came up through the floorboards on our bridge up to our chest. Though we wore immersion suits and thermal boots, after the first hour or so of a four-hour watch at night, our suits leaked enough to create the most miserable conditions I've ever experienced. We wore safety belts fastened to a fitting to prevent us from being swept overboard and certain death. These were definitely "Victory at Sea" conditions.

An important collateral duty was getting qualified in submarines, earning my gold dolphins, and getting the qualified insignia. When I reported aboard *Redfin*, I was issued a three-inch-thick qualifications notebook where I had to answer all technical questions and diagram most systems on the boat, plus demonstrate to my Captain that I could get the boat underway and dock it, dive and surface the boat, and conduct a successful periscope approach on a target ship without being detected.

When I became proficient in my knowledge of the systems and demonstrated my abilities to execute expected operations, my Captain nominated me for qualification. I then had an in-port qualification on another boat and an underway qualification on still an additional boat, where I had to conduct a submerged attack on a ship using the periscope among other tasks. Finally, I qualified and pinned on my gold dolphins, a significant accomplishment for me.

I soon became the Engineering Officer with the responsibility for the equipment, batteries, engines, and motors, and, most of all, men to operate and maintain them. I also had the additional duty to qualify all unqualified enlisted men on board. With these responsibilities, I interacted with most of the crew. After all these decades, I'm thrilled to be in contact with enlisted men and officers I served with—very special, smart, and talented men. We have attended most of the *Redfin* Reunions, which have been informal and located in various cities for fun activities.

As I think back to my time aboard *Redfin*, the boat went through several shipyard periods for major changes. Originally, the boat was designated SS during WWII, but after the war, the boat was cut in half and a thirty-foot section was added to accommodate new radar equipment. The new space was called Aircraft Control Center, ACC, and the boat designation was changed to SSR to signify its new mission as a radar-picket submarine. During the Cold War period, radar picket boats were stationed off our coasts to provide an early warning of the approach of enemy aircraft. This was the mission when I first reported aboard, but soon we found ourselves in the Philadelphia Naval Shipyard again to be re-equipped for another mission.

In the shipyard, radar equipment was removed, and the thirty-foot section was renamed Navigation Information Center, NIC, for the inertial navigation system that was installed along with secret equipment to be tested for the fleet ballistic missile boats soon to be joining our Navy. Our boat designation changed again, we were now AGSS, for auxiliary geological duty. We were moved out of the sub squadron in Norfolk and became a single boat in a squadron under the guise of staff in Washington, DC. We didn't see much of them.

Onboard activities at sea changed dramatically, and we soon began testing the new equipment with PhDs and equipment technicians from universities and major corporations who were monitoring and maintaining the new equipment for the *USS George Washington* (SSBN 598), the first fleet ballistic missile submarine, soon to be launched by the Electric Boat Company in Groton, Connecticut.

During the testing, some equipment was removed from time to time, and others were installed with a subsequent change of contractors who had to share a bunk with a crew member—hot bunking, we called it. During the year we spent as a pseudo-missile boat, we became the first boat to get into Cape Canaveral, to go on a missile patrol north of the Arctic Circle, and into the Royal Navy Submarine Base in Faslane, Scotland.

There, we side-tied up outboard of the British submarine, *HMS Narwhal*, which had—what do you think?—an imitation tusk, like one on a real narwhal, at the front of the bridge, of course. The Royal Navy officers invited us to a superb dinner affair at Loch Lomond Castle that evening, which was located a few miles away.

As the Engineering Officer on *Redfin*, I rode with my counter-part on the *Narwhal* in an open MG sports car on a trip where I truly believed I would die. Driving on the wrong side of the road at a very high speed on the hilly, winding road, could not have been more dangerous, which I believed was designed to make an impression on me. It did, I'll never forget it. My driver and new *Narwhal*-Engineering-Officer friend had the most impressive red beard you have ever seen, and an outgoing personality to go with it. It was a fun evening, though a little on the scary side. In true Royal navy tradition, the Queen picked up the tab for the food and drink.

I have a couple of events to share that aren't classified but might be of interest to the reader. We went into the Portsmouth, Virginia, Naval Shipyard to change out our forward battery, which I believed had been in the boat since WWII. Before we went into the yard, I tried to find someone who had changed out a submarine battery. No luck, I was on my own with my electricians.

Maintaining the two batteries on a submarine requires caution of course, and changing one out, in particular, is hard and dangerous work in very cramped quarters. Each lead-acid battery had 126 cells, and each cell weighed one ton. The process involved electrically disconnecting each cell and manhandling it beneath the hole cut in the hull for a crane to lift the cells out and put the new ones in. It was dangerous and required expertise that we were gaining as the process continued.

After we properly installed the new cells we learned were from a leftover WWII battery, we had to do a start-up charge for the battery. We began very cautiously and measured the specific gravity in the cells often to see if the charge was going into the batteries. At ten o'clock that evening, when the gravities were not coming up, I told my electricians to go home and get some rest. They were exhausted, and like me, concerned about the lack of progress of the charge which should have been completed hours ago; we stopped the charge to await more information.

The next morning, I called Exide, the battery manufacturer in Philadelphia, to reach someone for confirmation of what we were doing or to provide us with another direction to get this battery charged—which had been "asleep" for many years. We were delighted to hear that everything we were doing was correct, it would just take longer to get the initial charge in, much longer than normal. So, with confidence, we started up the charge again, and soon the specific gravities began rising until we had a fully charged battery. We were sure glad when that was over because battery problems on submarines had been the source of a few serious accidents over the years. Staying out of this accident history was definitely in the back of our minds.

As the official Diving Officer of the boat, I was on the dive at periscope depth, waiting to surface on one occasion we knew would be hazardous. Our batteries were low from staying submerged for many hours, dodging a hurricane above us with waves so strong, we were rolling fifteen degrees at two hundred feet deep. I had the boat trimmed light, keeping a downward angle on the boat to keep us from being sucked up to the surface by the giant waves. This technique worked well for me as I fought to maintain depth control. Our plan was to surface and get into

St. George's Harbor on Bermuda, which would provide a lee area away from the strongest wind. The Captain looked down from the conning tower, "Jim, are you ready?"

I replied, "Yes sir."

The surface alarm was sounded, and I blew the bow buoyancy tank to get the bow up and then the main ballast tanks. Up the ladder to the conning tower I went, and then, up the ladder to the bridge with the Quartermaster hanging on the ladder as well. I told him to crack the hatch and when no water came down, I had him open it. I raced up the rest of the way to see what we faced, the Captain right behind me. I started the low-pressure blowers to get the rest of the water out of the ballast tanks so we would float higher in the water.

In my conversation with the Captain, and watching wide-eyed at waves that appeared to be as tall as the Empire State Building, I lost track of the time blowing the ballast tanks empty. When the Captain told me to head into St. George's, I had the safety belts passed up to the bridge for my two lookouts and me to hook us to the bridge. Then I gave the order to change course and, without thinking, increased to two-thirds speed. Bad decision. Instead of going over the first wave after changing course, we went through it because we still had excess water in the ballast tanks.

With the first splash of water, the hatch was closed instantly to keep water out of the boat, but in the meantime, we were under deep water on the bridge. For a few seconds, I thought we would drown, but when we came out the other side of the wave, I called on the 20MC to the helmsman "all stop." No change, and then we went through the next wave. When we came out the other side of it, I used the 1MC, the ship-wide system, "all stop." I finally got a reaction to my order. One of my lookouts was hanging over the side by his safety line, and the other with a gash on his nose, helped me pull the lookout back aboard.

The Hell with this stuff, we moved down to the conning tower, and I notified the Captain that we were navigating from there, using the periscope, because it was too dangerous on the bridge. We made it into St. George's safely.

End of "sea stories," though there were more, they were not as eventful, thank goodness.

While we were at sea in *Redfin,* on one of our trips, I received a message from a classmate on another boat that Pat had delivered a beautiful baby boy. Our family was growing, and our son Tom had arrived and later served a few years in the Navy himself. Daughter Linda was born in Maryland a few years later. All three were born in different states. Pat was still counting moves and children.

Jim's Gold
Dolphins.

Jim on the
bridge of
Redfin in
heavy
weather.

USNA cup—Commander Nash presenting Jim
with a cup for winning the Brigade Intramural
Tennis Championship to the joy of others.

OVERBOARD WILLIE

THIS STORY IS THE MOST heart-tugging experience I have ever been involved in. It was a much more traumatic experience than watching a close, elderly family member die. Accidents resulting in death are events that should not be happening, but seeing one happen is real. It is happening right in front of you, and no matter what you do, it is not enough. That is the essence of this tragic story.

The *USS Redfin* (SS-272, SSR-272, AGSS-272, SS-272), as noted here, went through several rebirths over the years and had one of these designations, SSR-272 when I reported aboard. After World War II, many of the old diesel boats, including *Redfin*, were converted for other duties than going after enemy ships. And although our Navy was designing new boats, as submarines are called, for new duties and using nuclear power for propulsion, would take time.

In the case of *Redfin*, a boat that had a distinguished World War II wartime career, went into the Philadelphia US Naval Shipyard after the war, where the boat was cut in half, and a new section, thirty feet long, was added. The new section was called Aircraft Control Center because that was where the radar and other monitoring equipment were installed. The new designation as SSR-272 was to reflect the new mission, radar picket duty. Submarines, modified similarly, were stationed far offshore of both of our coasts to detect and report enemy planes approaching our country.

For further background, *Redfin* went back into the Philadelphia Naval Shipyard in April of 1959 to prepare the boat for a new assignment. The topside radar paraphernalia was removed, and new classified equipment was installed in the Aircraft Control Center, which was renamed Navigation Information Center. Our new duty was to test and evaluate the equipment that was expected to go on the *USS George Washington* (SSBN-598), our first Fleet Ballistic Missile submarine.

With the new equipment added, *Redfin* was ready for its next mission and was then detached from Submarine Squadron Six and began new operations under Submarine Squadron Fourteen headquartered in Washington, DC, the only boat in the new squadron. We got a lot of attention and support from "on high."

Another aspect of the new missile boats being added to the Navy Fleet was the need for more officers to man two crews on each one. Previously, because of the limited number of officers on subs, officers were required to spend a year at sea so that they came aboard a boat ready to take on multiple duties. To meet this increased requirement for more submarine officers, young, newly commissioned officers were sent directly to Submarine School from the Naval Academy or NROTC programs without a year of sea duty.

Willie Wilson graduated from Annapolis in 1960, went to Sub School for six months, and then reported aboard *Redfin* with very little time spent at sea and was not qualified for Officer of the Deck responsibilities. I remember Willie Wilson very vividly. He took to a rigorous training program on *Redfin* and impressed the other officers and crew with how quickly he learned his duties and soon was qualified to stand topside watches alone. Willie did have the benefit of serving for a short while as an enlisted man before he went to Annapolis and quickly became a favorite of the crew.

I had the midwatch (midnight to 4:00 a. m,) on the night of the overboard incident and went to my bunk after dinner, hoping to get a couple of hours of sleep before my watch. I don't remember the exact time, but it was still daylight, around 1900 (7:00 p.m.). The boat was hit by a big wave and immediately by another, it was a bang, bang, and the boat heeled over sharply. Almost at once, on the 1MC (the boat-wide speaker system) we heard, "Man overboard, the officer of the deck overboard." I jumped out of my bunk and into my sea boots and ran to the bridge as fast as I could. The Executive Officer, Bill Bourne, was just ahead of me. He climbed up on the turtleback on the back and above the bridge area, and I took the conn (control of boat operations).

Bill said, "There he is," and, we saw him briefly upon the top of a wave.

I immediately looked down into the conning tower and shouted, "Right full rudder, starboard back full, port ahead full." The helmsman repeated the command and executed them as I was determined to get to him quickly by twisting the boat into as tight of a turn as we could. When I looked up, he was not on top of the next wave. He was gone, but we looked for twenty-four hours with other boats and ships in the area.

I remember Rich O'Sullivan, who was Navigator at the time, calculated the drift factor as we looked. At some point, I was relieved on the bridge by the next watch, it got dark, and then we had a driving rainstorm. Awful, very sad experience. He didn't have a chance. He had on a thick parka and thermal boots which could have dragged him down too. As I recall, he was an excellent swimmer. When I talked to Mac, COB (chief of the boat), he mentioned that he may have hit his head on the tank top when he went overboard, which was very possible. I miss Mac—but that's another story.

In reviewing the facts, the radar operator down below had

reported a ship contact at around twenty thousand yards, and Willie was looking through either his binoculars or the TBT (target bearing transmitter) trying to locate the other ship when the huge wave hit him from behind. We don't think he ever saw it. We were lucky we didn't lose the two lookouts also who reported a man overboard as fast as they did. They did an excellent job, we all did everything we could to save him, but we didn't have a chance.

When the seas picked up, he could have asked the quartermaster to pass up the safety lines to tie themselves to the bridge, but I doubt if he even knew about them, and he may not have recognized the need. If that was a rogue wave, then sea conditions may not have warranted asking for them. Later, when I thought about the safety line issue, I didn't ask for them either when I took over the conn of the boat since I didn't see the need at the moment. We were busy—very busy—and I asked for our qualified swimmers to stand by and to bring up a throwable line to the bridge too.

The Norfolk operating areas for submarines had rough weather most of the time but not enough to require safety lines on the bridge. After this incident, we added a foot-tall railing around the bridge as a safety precaution, that was the only thing we did. No one was admonished for any lapse in any way. It was only a very sad, freak accident with everyone doing their duty very responsibly.

About fifteen years ago, the daughter who never knew her father, called me to hear the story. Her mother remarried very soon after Willie was lost, and her father's name never came up. She lived in Clemson, South Carolina, and we talked for about an hour, and though I told her to call me anytime she had any questions, I never heard from her again. Before our conversations with her, she knew nothing about her father but, hopefully, we (Jim Gradeless and several *Redfin* men) gave her enough information so she could pass it on to future family generations. We sent his name to be added to the Navy Memorial in Washington, DC, and for those of us on *Redfin* that fateful day, Willie Wilson will never be forgotten.

SUBMARINE SCHOOL GRADUATION REMARKS
May 30, 2014

U NKNOWN TO US, basic Submarine School classes were named after World War II boats at some point, and when our *Redfin* Reunion coordinator, Jim Martin, was contacted and asked for someone from our boat to make a few remarks at the *Redfin* class graduation ceremony, he asked me to do it. I agreed to do it if Erich Cramer, a fellow *Redfin* officer and good friend, would join me. Erich agreed, and we each decided to cover different subjects in our remarks, which we shared with each other after completing them.

Before the ceremony at the New London submarine base, we were met at the gate and escorted to the Sub School skipper's office. After exchanging pleasantries, I went into Anderson Hall, named after the first captain of the *Nautilus*, full of young sailors eagerly awaiting their graduation certificates and ready to begin the next phase of their Navy life.

Then I engaged a large group of them in conversation. When I asked them if they had read several books about submarine warfare in World War II, I was amazed when one of them had read them all. I was very impressed with these young men and talking with these men who truly hung on every word I said, was one of the most exhilarating moments of my life.

Then, the chief came into the room and grabbed me by the arm, saying, "We need to go out into the hall to line up to march into the room." For an eighty-one-year-old, it never occurred to me that we would march into the main hall. Erich's wife was saving seats for us in the front row, but when we entered the room, we were led up on the stage not knowing what would come next.

The day was full of surprises for us. On the stage, were the Commanding Officer of the Submarine School, Captain Jarrett, Master Chief Schultz, the Chaplain, a representative of the World War II Veterans Association, Erich, and me. When I was introduced, I looked at my notes briefly, but never again—I knew exactly what I was going to say.

"Captain Jarrett, Master Chief Schultz, guests, family, and graduates: Thank you for inviting Erich and me to be with you today. We served on the *Redfin*, the 272 boat, in the late '50s and early '60s.

"Congratulations from the men who served on the *Redfin*, and on their behalf, Erich and I install you as new members of the crew. When you get a chance, look up your new boat on the website if you haven't already done so.

"Erich and I will give you a brief history of *Redfin*, and our thoughts for this very significant day in your lives."

Erich gave his remarks and then I continued:

"For those family members and those that do not know the background of this storied boat, here are a few things you might want to know. On the second war patrol in 1944, under Skipper Cy Austin, Redfin sank five Japanese ships, a destroyer, three cargo ships, and an oiler—quite an achievement. After the war, the boat was assigned to various missions, first as a radar picket boat offshore to provide an alert that enemy airplanes were approaching our country. When Erich and I were aboard, the boat had a different mission. We evaluated equipment designed for the missile boats, soon to join the fleet. That equipment evolved into that used on the missile boats today.

"Today is a day that you have long-awaited. You are a submariner for life, a remarkable achievement, and speaking for the *Redfin* Crew, we are very proud of you and thank you for volunteering to join the submarine service, a select Navy organization.

"Here are our wishes and challenges for you:

"First and foremost, get qualified. The day you pin on your Dolphins will be another very special day. When you report aboard your boat and your new department, you'll stand watches, and work on your qualifications. Everyone on board will not only be interested in your qualification status but will help you in every step of the process. When a department or compartment signs off on your qualification sheet, that person is really signing off that he is placing his life in your hands. The silver Dolphins are something so special, you will cherish them for the rest of your life.

"Second, work hard. Make chief and help the young sailors, that's important. The chiefs are the backbone of the Navy and continuing the training of the young men in your division will be your responsibility. One chief I'll never forget is Chief Shorty Metzger, who taught marlinspike seamanship to us during our first summer at Annapolis, but rope tying is not what I remember. His words of wisdom were very meaningful, for example, 'You can put stripes on a jackass, but that doesn't make him an officer. Listen to your chiefs.'

"Third, let's see, have you seen the movie *City Slickers* with Billy Crystal and Jack Palance, who won an Oscar for this role in the movie? Three New Yorkers, in a midlife crisis, go out west on vacation to join other dudes on a cattle drive to bring a herd of cattle home from a distant pasture, a multi-day adventure. Jack Palance played the role of the ramrod on the drive—he was scary, terrifying to all the dudes. With the big knife he carried, the dudes were sure he would cut their throats one night. Unapproachable really, but one day, he asked Billy Crystal to ride out with him to find a stray to bring back to the herd. Billy Crystal went with him, expecting the worse, but the comedian tried to probe Jack Palance to lighten him up a little to find out who he really was. Jack Palance, turned around on his horse and said, 'The secret to life is one thing,' while holding up one finger [which I did too].

"Billy Crystal says 'Your finger?'

"With a big smile, Jack Palance replies, 'No, that's for you to figure out.'

"For me, that one thing is relationships. So, the third thing that our crew asked us to convey to you, is for you to create relationships with your shipmates, as we have done, to last YOU a lifetime. Create relationships with your wife, your family, your school classmates, and friends too. Nurture those relationships and for sure, you will have a happy life.

"Finally, have dreams about your future. Experience is something you get every day, but dreams take planning and courage. Don't be afraid to pursue them.

"I have two examples for you; A Naval Academy 1957 classmate of mine, Ken Malley, started out as a seaman recruit in the Navy, just like you. His dream was to go to Annapolis. He pushed, worked for it, got in, graduated, went into the fleet, made three stars, became a Vice-Admiral. If he could do it, so can you. We had over 150 classmates at the Academy in my class who came from the fleet.

"The second example is a different Navy career path. Mike Gordon, a friend and neighbor, was a seaman recruit as well. Wherever he was stationed, he attended college—the University of Connecticut, University of Michigan, University of Hawaii, Old Dominion, and three others. He went to supply school and Sub School as an officer and retired after thirty-eight years in the Navy as a captain. If Mike could do it, so could you.

"Whatever your dreams might be, go for it. You have already achieved a major step in your life by graduating from Sub School.

And we are very proud of you, your families are proud of you, and your instructors are proud of you. Keep up the good work submariners. Oh, and one other thing, if you get down to Kings Bay, look me up, I'll take you bass fishing."

Big smiles!

Then, I was surprised again when I was directed to go over to the side of the stage next to a second-class petty officer, who had the graduation certificates, and to give them out after Master Chief Schultz read their names. The young men were lined up, one row at a time, standing at attention, ready to come up on the stage. As each man came up, I shook his hand and gave him his certificate, but most of all, I tried to comment to each of them to make them smile. What an unexpected honor that was.

After the ceremony, I went down to talk with the class some more, it was so delightful to interact with these very smart young men about to embark on a submarine career. The young man who graduated first in his class was very special, but when I asked him what he was going to do that afternoon, he climbed into my heart when he said, "I'm going bass fishing." What a thrill that day was. We went on a tour of the base and had lunch with a group of chief petty officers.

After I got home, Pat said I was walking two feet off the ground. I had been through an amazing experience. At the next *Redfin* reunion, our shipmates wanted us to say the remarks for them, which we did. Can you believe it? A standing ovation! Our men at the reunion were so proud! Later, I was asked to repeat my remarks at an American Legion meeting, where I received applause. The entire experience was not only worthwhile but one so special to me, words cannot express how special it was for this ancient mariner. Wow!

Jim handing
out diplomas
at Sub School
graduation
with Erich
Cramer
looking on.

Jim speaking
to the
graduating
group at Sub
School with
Erich Cramer
looking on.

Afterword

THINGS WE DID TOGETHER

———

LTHOUGH THESE ARE NOT stories as in the primary
content of the book, it would be remiss not to mention a few
of the significant projects completed by committed groups of
people. Describing these is a way for me to recognize what we
accomplished together. It was an honor to work with so many
people, donating so much time and effort to work these projects
together, and, more importantly, to build relationships to last a
lifetime. Thanks again for all of the help and sacrifice that you en-
dured to accomplish so much.

Gillnet Initiative

If I had to select the most important project we ever completed,
this one would be near the top of the list because of the effort required from so many people in a very short period of time. Those
two words in the title likely have no meaning for most people who
read these accounts, so, let me explain.

Gillnets can be of various mesh sizes and lengths, but they

form a wall in the ocean that entrap fish when they swim into them by tangling their gill area in the net so they can't get out. When they are placed perpendicular to a beach or island, schools of fish that generally swim parallel to the land are trapped with no escape. Also trapped are marine mammals like sea lions and sharks too that feed on the trapped fish. The nets are indiscriminate in what is ensnared, and the number of fish killed is unlimited to the degree that some species of fish have been almost wiped out in countries that don't regulate them.

In California, the prized sportfish white seabass, a member of the croaker family, was being impacted severely by over-harvesting in what was perceived to be an indiscriminate manner. Recreational fishermen were concerned that if gillnets were not eliminated, the species would be more seriously impacted. Thus, Assemblywoman Doris Allen was sponsoring a signature campaign to place an initiative on the next ballot to eliminate gillnets as a means of fishing in California waters defined as three miles from the mainland and one mile from islands. Based on the number of voters in the last election, about 550,000 "qualified" voter signatures would be required to get it on the ballot so that California voters could decide this issue since the state legislature would not. "Qualified voters" meant ones that were registered to vote.

Since only six months were allowed to get these signatures turned in and validated, a monumental effort would be required to get them.

In the meantime, I had been asked to help organize a concerned group called the Gillnet Watch Committee, an eclectic group of men and women, all connected to fishing in one way or another. When the clock started ticking on the six-month time period, and people were concerned that this effort was doomed to failure, a couple of members of the watch committee went to Assemblywoman Allen and told her that new leadership was urgently needed. She asked me, as requested by a group of fishermen who knew my background in management. In turn, I asked the Gillnet Watch Committee if they would essentially put their lives on hold for the next five months (one month was over) to be the leadership group for this effort. When they agreed, I accepted the challenge.

There was no way a volunteer effort would be enough to obtain around 625,000 signatures needed in order to get the 550,000 "validated" ones, since we knew that some people not registered to vote would sign petitions, sign their names incorrectly, signed more than once, etc. We quickly put together and staffed an office with volunteers to answer the phone and mail out posters and petitions and began an all-out effort to create the perception of success, a key detail to get the money to hire a professional company to hire people to gather signatures while we volunteers did also.

Without going into much detail, fishermen across the state took petitions everywhere. They put them on charter boats, walked the fishing piers, stood at the gates of major events, manned the booths at fishing shows, and county fairs. We were everywhere. We busted our butts!

When it was time for us to turn in the volunteer signatures, we did it in such a way as to create major media events. In a donated twin-engine airplane that carried a group of us and fast enough to cover the state in one day, we set up presentations to celebrate the completion of our effort. We left Orange County Airport, located south of Los Angeles, before daylight and made the long trip to Sacramento for an event in the governor's media room, where it was packed. Next, we ate lunch on the plane as we headed south to Burbank, where many VIPs would attend along with several TV stars. It was packed with people and TV cameras, as it was in Sacramento. When it was over, we headed for San Diego where the fishing clubs were going to drive fork trucks loaded with pallets of petitions to put on the steps of the courthouse. This was a fun effort that attracted a crowd and more TV cameras.

When we arrived back at the Orange County Airport, it was dark, but we managed to cover the state and not only get the signatures turned in on time but did it in a way to get the maximum TV coverage. Finally, we had to sweat out the signature count!

Later, we learned our effort was successful, and the Gillnet Initiative would be on the ballot as Proposition 132. With more effort, we did more events for more TV coverage. Then election night, Bill Ray sponsored an election night event at the prestigious Balboa Bay Club he owned, where the invited guests nervously watched the count come in. We were ahead all night and won a decisive victory for recreational anglers. Gillnets in California waters were phased out over three years. We got it done!

White Seabass Project

With the success of the Gillnet Initiative, we were asked to take over a new fishing conservation organization, United Anglers of Southern California, which we built into one of the largest ones in the country doing legislation and projects. A favorite was one that involved the Department of Fish and Game, Sea World, Business, and fishing clubs from San Diego to Santa Barbara. White seabass tended to swim parallel to the beach and the fish were easy victims of the nets, but with the nets gone, we could expand a program started at Sea World in San Diego to raise white seabass for release into the ocean, but with an added kick to the program.

The Hubbs Sea World Research Institute reached an agreement with San Diego Gas and Electric to lease seven and a half acres of land on a lagoon in Carlsbad, just north of San Diego for a nominal fee, a donation of the land really. Now we needed to raise money to build the hatchery and the first two people that we called pledged $50,000 each. We were on the way. After attending many Carlsbad City Council meetings and satisfying neighbors' concerns, we were granted a permit to build the hatchery.

Needing money to operate the hatchery, we wrote legislation to put a three-dollar stamp on fishing licenses to cover this expense. Without going into every detail, we organized fishing club boats to catch adult white seabass to use as the brood stock for the hatchery on organized trips to Catalina Island. These fish were placed into a special tank on a boat with hatchery workers to see that they were properly handled. All of us including the experts went through a learning process.

These adult fish became the "mommas and daddies" for the hatchery and were replaced regularly to diversify the released fish population. The California Department of Fish and Game appointed a representative to be the advisor for the program, and we were told that if we could release fish ten to twelve inches in length, the survival rate would be much greater than the four-inch fish coming out of the hatchery.

Fishing clubs volunteered to build grow-out pens to raise the smaller fish up to a release size of the recommended ten to twelve inches. The delivery of fish to the pens and release of the larger fish became major media events and feeding and tending the pens is still going on today, twenty-five years later. Millions of fish have been released because of this effort by so many organizations and volunteers.

The marine biology department at California State University, Northridge collects the heads turned into them by fishermen via various means. The fish found with a coded wire tag inserted into each fish's gill plate that was raised in the program could now be read. The data analyzed is reported to everyone and it's interesting to note that the fish migrated to offshore islands and back to the mainland but didn't go very far north or south into Mexico.

We have learned so much about the white seabass since beginning this program and building one of the most sophisticated hatcheries in the world. As I said, this complex group of dedicated people prove that people will work together if the goal is a worthy one, and this one has been exactly that. Incredibly, a recent genetics study showed that the hatchery program has been a highly successful one with as many as thirty per cent of caught white sea bass are raised and tagged in the Hubbs-Sea World Research Institute Hatchery.

Artificial Reefs

Before I was involved in fishing conservation, another member of Huntington Harbour Anglers called me to discuss the removal of the Huntington Beach pier, which had been severely damaged in a storm. "Why couldn't the concrete be used as an artificial reef?" I didn't know anything about artificial reefs, but I knew someone who did, Russ Izor, who ran a fishing boat for recreational anglers.

After his agreement to help me, I went before the city council and asked for their agreement to use the pier concrete to dump into a designated reef area about nine miles off the coast in ninety-two feet of water. I agreed to raise the $25,000 to complete the project with no idea where I would get the money. However, I was saved from possible embarrassment when the California Dept. of Fish and Game tested the one-hundred-year-old concrete and deemed it to be unsuitable for reef material.

The takeaway from this attempt was that we had developed a relationship with Dennis Bedford, who was the head of the reef program for the California Department of Fish and Game.

Later, when I was leading a fishing conservation group, one of our first projects was building artificial reefs. Once we let it be known we could take concrete material out to the reef area, our phone started ringing. We coordinated truckloads of concrete to arrive at thirty-minute intervals because we only had the flat barge for one day of loading and the dump day. Various items were donated to us, concrete sound wall panels, concrete fireplaces with the chimney stack attached, concrete from docks being replaced, huge concrete pipe, and clean concrete rubble from construction sites.

One day, we received a call from Southern California Edison to ask us if we could use concrete streetlight poles on the reef.

I asked, "How many do you have?"

"Thousands."

"Wow, where did all of these come from?"

"Mostly knockdowns from cars running into them," Southern California Edison replied. They were paying big-time storage fees all over Los Angeles for them, and they could save money by giving them to us. Mutual benefit!

We arranged to get a huge mud barge that was designed to take dredging material out to a designated site, called a dead zone, and to open the bottom to dump it without any effect on sea life. The day before the dump, we took Dennis, DFG, out to the site where he wanted to place the streetlight poles and placed a temporary buoy with a light on it to keep it safe until the next day. When the tug left the breakwater area the next morning, he called us on the radio to give us a progress report. So, we knew about when he would arrive with the barge.

The dump procedure is fun to watch because the tug must stop the barge exactly at the buoy with no brakes to use. Here's how it's done: the tug with the tow makes a U-turn around the buoy and stops it at exactly the right place. Perfectly done, and the tug held the barge in place until all the poles had fallen out of the barge when the bottom was opened like a clamshell. In a matter of a few minutes, the poles were on the bottom, and the tug was headed home. Incidentally, SCE sent an airplane out to take some photos for advertising purposes, and I have one of the large photos over my desk. The best dump we ever had.

On a previous dump, we had a little extra attention in the process. We routinely sent notices to the media so that other boaters who wanted to observe the dump could plan to do so. Typically, the media joined us on boats we designated for them. And so, it was not unusual to receive a call after an article about the dump appeared in the LA Times to request a boat ride out to the dumpsite.

However, when Jim Hill, Los Angeles Bureau Chief for CNN, called, he not only wanted to watch the dump, but he also wanted to send two divers down to get footage of the material on the bottom and to do the same at a dump from a previous year to see the growth on that material and the fish on the reef. Routinely, a caterpillar tractor pushed the concrete material off both sides of the barge in a fascinating manner stopping the tractor inches before it followed the material off the barge. To me, the cat driver looked like an artist at work, an incredible job.

Oh yeah, one other thing. Jim Hill wanted to dive on the reef site too. Oh boy, the last thing that I wanted was for the CNN Bureau Chief to die during this event. Ninety-two feet of water requires extra qualification and can be dangerous. However, a fishing buddy and world-class diver, Ron Moss, agreed to supervise the dive and took us out on his thirty-seven-foot boat. We made it very clear to the CNN crew that Ron would be in charge and could stop the dive if anything went awry. Everything went well and TV coverage of the event was televised on CNN all over the world for a week.

Grace Lutheran Church

While I was treasurer at Grace Lutheran Church in Huntington Beach, the subject came up at a board meeting regarding the upcoming ten-year anniversary of the young church. The discussion was about things we might do as a part of the celebration. From the management of the books and paying all the bills, I knew we were barely surviving financially. I also knew we desperately needed to get out of the rut and grow the church.

When I suggested a fundraising program to make needed improvements, I was told that the budget was set and voted on by the congregation and could not be changed. However, I finally convinced them to let me talk with the congregation about raising $25,000 to replace the folding chairs with pews in the sanctuary, paving the back area where cars got stuck in the mud after a rainstorm, and buying a piano for the Sunday School. The cost would be about two hundred dollars per member. We did it and in turn, demonstrated that this young church was growing, not failing.

Later, while I served as president of the congregation, we raised $200,000 to build a multipurpose building that had folding walls that could turn eight classrooms into a single room for potluck dinners, and it had a commercial kitchen that could serve out a window opening to the patio for coffee and donuts after church. Wonderful fellowship opportunity.

Next, we raised over a million dollars to build a beautiful new sanctuary, designed by one of the best church architects in the country. Then we raised funds to turn the old sanctuary into a two-story building for classrooms, offices, and a teenage game room. Over a ten-year period, we had transformed a minor church in the area into one with great programs for all age groups and a school K–6 grade.

Still, later, we reached an agreement with the local school board to move our school into an unused elementary school nearby to reduce the wear and tear on our church complex.

Together, we clearly demonstrated what we could do if we were willing to make sacrifices and work toward a common goal.

Barge—Dredge spoils barge filled with concrete telephone poles beginning to open at the reef site. *Kingfisher* in the background.

Jim Donlon who started grow pen concept at the Ventura grow-out pen.

Jim at Gillnet Initiative Election night party with the
current vote displayed—we won!

Acknowledgments

S O MANY PEOPLE helped me in so many ways to put this book together, and I will always be grateful for their efforts to make it the best it can be. Thanks, and more thanks.

Shawn Arnold, Bill Baab, Winn Baker, Doug Bannister, Pete and Eleanor Boyne, David Brazell, Bart Campbell, Erich Cramer, Tim Duchene, Hono Elizalde, Carol and Mark Fipps, Terry Foreman, Bud Galli, Beckie Gowen, Jim Gradeless, Charlie Hall, Melanie Johnsen, Norman Johnson, Tom Marnane, Dorothy Paulk McClain, Jim Martin, Pam Minor, Tom Paulk, Barbara Perry, George Larry (Dazy) Perry, Teresa Readdick, Dan Roper, Pete Thomas, Nanci Tisman, Barbara Williams, Julian Williams, Dr. Glenn Tisman, and, of course, my new friends and partners at BookLogix.

Writing this book has been a long, hard process for an old man (young at heart!), but to me, it has been worth it and hopefully for you.

Jim with an 11.33-pound sheepshead caught on Justin Paulk's boat.

Bob Clark with a rare Short-bill spearfish caught on *Kingfisher*.

Jim touring a group of NATO naval officers on a *Redfin* VIP cruise.

Jim and Bob McNary with East Coast family visitors. L–R: Bob McNary, Jim, Tom Paulk, Grandpa Jimmy Paulk, Bobby Paulk, and kneeling, Skip Paulk with his first marlin.

Jim and Pat

Back: Tom and Veronica Paulk; Second row: Rocky and Linda Readick, Pam and John Minor.

Pat with their three children, Linda, Tom, and Pam.

Pat and Jim with his three siblings, Bobby, Beckie, and Dorothy.

Good friend Bill Baab, teasing and pretending to eat a replica of George Perry's big bass.

Jim with a keeper redfish.

Pat and Jim
with their four
grandchildren,
Meagan,
Dylan,
Melanie, and
the oldest,
Jennifer.

Gathering
water for the
Ring Dance
ceremony on a
submarine.

PIC of the WEEK
AT LAST

Here is the Gulf of Siam's contribution to the Ring
Dance Ceremony. One of the seven pints of sea water
gathered, one from each of the seven seas, for the
ring ceremony was collected by LTJG Louis Frad on
board the Rasher, a radar picket submarine. This
water will go into 1957's landmark so that the Seven
Seas will be represented when the Dregs dip those
rings in the water before giving them to the Second
Class to wear for the first time.

Pat in her Navy
jacket exposing
her Delaware
sweatshirt at the
fiftieth reunion
Navy/Delaware
football game—
Delaware won!

Submarine
Redfin,
picture
courtesy of
Norman
Johnson.

Pen—White
seabass
grow-out
pen in
Ventura,
California,
harbor.

Pen—Grow-
out pen with
automatic
feeder hung
over it.

Pat receiving
award from
admiral.

Mark Garner,
former pro
fisherman, a
neighbor, with
the best of
their day.

Dennis
Patterson
with the best
of our day.

Pat and Jim
dancing
together,
which we
always loved
doing.

Scope—Jim at the periscope with quartermaster on the left and Captain Poteet on the right grading the procedure.

Army—Jim at North Georgia College.

Our offshore sportfishing boat, *Kingfisher*, was the scene of many years of fishing adventures for the family.

Irv Friedman rigging an aluminum jig for casting on *Kingfisher*.

Though Pat loved to dress up, sometimes we'd catch a moment of her letting her hair down and relaxing! Here she is on *Kingfisher* with Jim in Avalon Bay, Catalina Island.

Avalon Bay and the casino where the broadcast of the big bands went nationwide in the background. Photo taken from the Wrigley mansion on the mountain.

Jim and Earl Piper, his Annapolis roommate, at his father's residence in the Naval Gun Factory, Washington, DC.

Pat and mooring partner, Nancy Tisman, having fun on the *Kingfisher*.

Pat and Melanie Tisman laughing it up on the *Kingfisher*'s ladder to flybridge in Avalon Bay on Catalina Island.

Linda Paulk with Melanie Tisman swinging on *Kingfisher*'s ladder to the flybridge in Avalon Bay on Catalina Island.

Jim's favorite lily,
Scheherazade,
one of hundreds
of flowers
planted in his
yard.

Jim plebe year.